£3.00

Any book
is can

P

Treatise on Asthma

The Medical Writings of

MOSES MAIMONIDES

❀❀❀❀❀❀❀❀❀

Treatise on Asthma

Edited by

SUESSMAN MUNTNER

Philadelphia and Montreal

J. B. LIPPINCOTT COMPANY

The acquisition of these manuscripts
and the research thereon
culminating in the translation
of the first volume
was made possible
through the generosity of
The Renowned Medical Scientist
and Great Friend of Humanity

THEODORE K. LAWLESS, M.D.

Chicago, Illinois

Physician, Scientist and Humanitarian

PREFACE

BÉLA SCHICK, M.D.

Maimonides, born in Cordova in 1135, was educated by his father and in medicine by Arabic teachers. When a young man of 28 years he settled in Cairo and soon was recognized as the greatest authority on Biblical interpretation. Famed as a philosopher, his treatise "The Guide for the Perplexed" vividly depicts his astounding wisdom.

As if this were not enough to assure him a place amongst the immortals, he was also a celebrated physician. His medical works, consisting of ten manuscripts all written in Arabic, have been resting in most of the great libraries of Europe, among them in the Papal Library in Rome. Realizing that these medical works of Maimonides must surely contain valuable information and translated, would reveal enlightment to the medical profession, it, therefore, was decided to undertake this arduous commitment.

The tremendous task of translating these Medical Manuscripts has been commenced, edited by Dr. Suessman Muntner and published by "ITRI," the Israel Torah Research Institute. Volume I of this first English Edition now appears—*The Book On Asthma*. After about fifteen years living in Cairo Maimonides was appointed to be the physician of the court of Saladin as of Saladin's son and successor who was afflicted with Asthma. Thereupon Maimonides was requested to give the Prince instructions as to the management of this disease.

When a philosopher has already attained fame during his lifetime, has been admired by thousands of people, and acclaimed an immortal by many, we can be certain that he must have been indeed an outstanding individual. We find Maimonides' writings were placed in the library of the Popes for safe keeping and have been lying there for many centuries. We can now realize in what high esteem they were held. This volume on Asthma, written in Arabic, intended as a guide for the son of Sultan Saladin, deserves to be translated into English. Thus making it available for the first time to the medical profession so that physicians of today may learn how extensive was the knowledge of this eminent 12th century scientist.

When I heard of the existence of the medical writings of Maimonides I became curious and looked forward to the time when I, as a physician, would be able to read the ideas that Maimonides held concerning Asthma and other medical problems. The reading of the manuscript was an exciting and rewarding experience. I was impressed by the depth of Maimonides' knowledge of the disease, by the clarity of the discussion of its cause and of the influence of the environment, as well as the general health of the individual upon the disease. Maimonides knew much about the diet to be recommended to asthma sufferers and he knew that certain foods increased their suffering. He studied drugs in connection with their therapeutic qualities. He perceived that the air of Cairo, as compared to the air of Alexandria, was more helpful to the Prince in helping him recover from his asthmatic attacks.

Maimonides fully appreciated the varying manifestations of the disease, and found that a comprehensive study necessitates consideration of its various phases. Therefore, he divided his dissertation into twelve chapters before writing a summary of his ideas. He discussed the subjects in great detail, giving special consideration to the patient's personality. His discussion of the proper diet included suggestions concerning the preparation of the food, the appropriate quantity to be eaten, the number of meals, and the importance of the fluid intake; the ill effect caused by over-eating and by the consumption of excessive fat. Maimonides also emphasized the importance of emotional problems, occupation, and the influence of sufficient sleep and rest, of massage and sexual excitement on the asthmatic state.

It is a great pleasure and a privilege and most enlightening to read this distinguished physician's discussions contained in his manuscript on Asthma. It is fascinating for a physician of the 20th century to realize what a vast knowledge this medical genius had acquired 800 years ago. Maimonides most certainly must elicit our greatest admiration and respect for his comprehensive medical observations and phenomenal philosophical works.

INTRODUCTION

M. MURRAY PESHKIN, M.D.

This volume is of interest to the entire medical world, but it is of special interest to the physicians in the United States and Canada. In these countries the field of allergic diseases has had to develop, perforce, because of the nature of the rapid industrialization and the presence of a fall weed pollen season. The weed pollens produce an overwhelming allergic response in millions of inhabitants of North America. This is in sharp contrast to the absence of a weed pollen season and therefore a smaller incidence of allergic diseases in almost all other areas of the world. The widespread clinical problem of North America has catalyzed laboratory research attested to by thousands of scientific investigations and two national allergy societies, the American Academy of Allergy and the American College of Allergists (whose memberships total approximately 1,500 individual physicians). National and regional allergy meetings uphold the level of investigative, teaching and clinical studies sponsored both spiritually and financially by a national lay philanthropic health organization: The Allergy Foundation of America. In spite of spectacular modern advances made in the theoretical and practical aspects of the allergies, the studies of the asthmatic state, written in the 12th century by Maimonides still merit our attention.

Maimonides states clearly that "asthma has many etiological aspects and should be treated according to the various causes that bring it about" . . . . and . . . . "the success of relieving the patient from asthma

xi

depends largely on an intimate knowledge of the *total* patient." To the latter prophetic statement he adds, "I have no magic cure to report." Do we have one today?

This volume on asthma was a command code of instructions covering hygiene, diet, medication, travel and personal behavior for the son and successor of Sultan Saladin of Egypt whose asthma, when he was 40 years of age, was initiated by the common cold and perennial allergic rhinitis. The latter condition also was separate and distinct from the asthmatic attacks.

The Prince, who lived in Alexandria, found he could tide over an asthmatic attack more quickly and easily by going to Cairo. Maimonides attributed this favorable response to the cleaner air in Cairo as contrasted to the contaminated air of populated Alexandria. In terms of our present experiences this reminds us of a possible change of a human, rather than an allergenic environment, which is implicit in Maimonides' observation that success in freeing a patient from asthma involves a thorough knowledge of the *total* patient. Maimonides took great trouble to stress the emotional aspects of asthma. But he also emphasized the value of special diets as we do today. He remarks, interestingly, that dietary measures are to be used in all disorders marked by *"seizures,"* such as inflammation of the joints, migraine and asthma. Today these conditions, among other "seizures," are largely involved with the allergic phenomenon.

Heredity is implied by Maimonides by his reference to the "bodily organs weak from birth." He stated that when the intestinal tract is not adversely affected by food, then the food itself "moves to less resistant organs where they settle down and aggravate the condition. If the organ is profoundly involved it may lead to death." This aptly describes "shock" organ hypersensitivity.

Maimonides advocated early treatment for the asthmatic patient because of the danger of ensuing organic complications and intractable asthma. He noted that when a patient did not respond well to the initial program of treatment, he searched for multiple causes.

Maimonides' discussion of air and psychic moods calls attention to cold, humidity and extremes of dryness and excess moisture as being very harmful. He notes that mental suffering impairs physical well being and adversely affects the respiratory organs; and this was universally known in the 12th century. He also credits the philosophers and psychologists with uncovering the nature of the mental condition and so being able to help the patient understand his problem.

"Mere diet and medical treatment cannot fully cure this disorder." This statement is in keeping with Maimonides' consistent adherence to the importance of the need to know intimately the "total patient." He adds, "sleep during an attack of asthma may be harmful." Today this advice is reminiscent of the dangers of oversedating a patient in the throes of a severe attack of asthma with drugs which tend to depress the respiratory center in the brain. He recommends avoidance of excessive bathing and of exposure to sudden changes in temperature—all recognized today as contributing nonspecific factors of asthma.

Food recipes are clearly outlined. It is, however, of interest to note that the foods restricted in the diet for asthmatic patients include fermented cheeses, most legumes, certain nuts, leek, onion, garlic, mutton, duck, goose, fatty foods, salty fish, the cabbage family, the melon family, peaches, grapes, berries, dates and certain species. What could better parallel the almost routine dietary restrictions prescribed for most asthmatic patients today?

Maimonides speaks of the use of preventive measures and "next comes the care for the cleansing of the lungs," for "every organ as a rule does away with bad residue when it regains its normal mixture thereby enhancing its functioning power." This kind of thinking has great meaning today. A description of the drugs used in asthma while "outside of the scope of the present book," nevertheless, did advocate a number of drugs designed to prevent the sputum from becoming "hardened, sticky and difficult to discharge. In any case, moisture content in such remedies should be pronounced to ease expectoration." Maimonides preferred to use a single drug in treatment and the use of the drug should be based "on authoritative sources."

Careful sickness-history taking was considered most important. Allergy tests, notwithstanding, this advice has a psychological implication, for a long history of the course of asthma has psychotherapeutic value. The following were some of the remedies mentioned: Enemas, smelling herbs "to dry out any humidity in the head." The draining of "juices" from the brain strongly implies the decongestion of the paranasal sinuses and the clearing of mucus from the nasopharyngeal and oropharyngeal areas. The goal of treatment was to clear the lungs of moisture, ease respiration and banish the cough. "Of all remedies there are no more perilous than blood letting and purgatives, next come emetics and strong enemas." However, strong medications prescribed by a physician at the right time for special cases on an individual basis may be helpful. Maimonides followed the teachings of Hippocrates, Galen and El-Razi but selected what he thought was useful. He spoke of the modern doctors of his time in terms of those discarding much of the teaching of the past because it was "unscientific." He clearly recognized the clinical relation between natural resistance and disease. When resistance is high, there is no disease and no need for medicine and vice versa.

Maimonides dwells at length on the psychological motivation of the true physician and warns against the bad physician and the elusive term "experience" as used by the ill-trained and ignorant physicians and quacks. He contends that training in the art of medicine consists most often of a combination of practice and theory. He makes a most up-to-date, intelligent and incontrovertable statement that "the physician should not treat the *disease* but the *patient* who is suffering from it." Maimonides had a special medicinal concoction which greatly relieved his asthmatic patients. What was the psychotherapeutic role that Maimonides played? Was there perhaps some form of automatic psychotherapy involved with the action of his asthma-relieving medication? Today allergists, psychologically oriented, may structure their psychotherapy. They are careful to avoid disturbing their patients. In most instances the allergist is best suited to give supportive therapy to asthmatic patients. A significant and meaningful suggestion by Maimonides to the Prince was: "'Let your Highness occupy himself with things useful and keep away from things useless and may God show you the path of truth."

Maimonides approved of consultations with specialists, because "they remind and assist each other to arrive at the desired end and so the best medical treatment is assured by use of the collegium." Maimonides' approach to the management of asthma is refreshing and it should serve to make one a more humble and more dedicated physician. It also should remind the reader of this book to carefully study Maimonides' thinking about the physician and his role in the practice of medicine. To quote: "It should be clear that medicine is a science essential to man, anytime, anywhere, not only in time of illness but in health as well. It truly can be said that medicine should be a man's constant companion. To be sure, this holds good only in the case of a consummate physician with a complete mastery of theoretical and practical knowledge, so that a man may safely lodge himself in his hands, body and soul, to be guided by his directions. Such physicians are encountered in all countries and in all times." He continues to remind us today with wisdom conceived in the 12th century, that "the clever, skilled physician who is versed in the fundamentals of medicine and thinks twice before he decides how to bring about a patient's relief, such a man always relies on the work of nature and keeps her from going lazy."

After reading this book we cannot escape from the feeling that we have relearned many things besides affording us a better and clearer perspective of the meaning of medicine to the great physicians of 800 or more years ago. What could be more psychologically stimulating, inspiring and even exciting to conclude my preface with Maimonides' quotation from the sages: "Love and hate lead judgment astray."

MAIMONIDES THE PHYSICIAN

MORRIS FISHBEIN, M.D.

Two great minds combined in the brain of one human—the contemplative mind of the philosopher; the scientific analysing mind of the physician. Maimonides wrote vigorously on astronomy, medicine, logic, liturgy, philosophy and the religious law. George Sarton called him one of the two greatest philosophers of his time. "The Guide of the Perplexed" which he wrote in Arabic was translated into Hebrew with Maimonides' advice in the year of his death and during the first half of the thirteenth century also into Latin. This great work is still studied in modern times. In his introduction to it Maimonides said: "The design of this work is to promote the true understanding of the real spirit of the Law, to guide those religious persons who, adhering to the Torah, have studied philosophy and are perplexed by the seeming contradictions between the teachings of philosophy and the literal sense of the Torah."

Maimonides was born in Cordova, Andalusia, in southern Spain, March 30, 1135. He came of a family of doctors. His father was a judge in Cordova, a learned man. The boy studied under his father and also with Rabbi ibn Migas. When still in his twenties he wrote essays and commentaries on religious subjects. A Muslim sect called Almohade invaded Cordova. To preserve their lives members of the Maimonides family had to choose between Islam and exile. They traveled about in Spain and went to Fez in Morocco in 1160. A few years later in 1165 they moved on to old Cairo. In that year the father died and for a brief period

Maimonides was involved with his brother David in a venture involving the buying and selling of jewelry. When this brother died at sea Maimonides, who had been studying medicine, became a physician.

According to the biography of Maimonides written by Solomon Zeitlin, Maimonides fled from Fez to Acco where he lived for a while. He visited the graves of the patriarchs at Hebron. During this time he was engaged in writing a commentary on the Mishna, in which he codified and explained the Jewish laws. From Acco he went to Alexandria and then in 1171 to Fostat, or old Cairo.

Among the philosophical writings of Maimonides are not only the Guide of the Perplexed but also a treatise on the art of logic, essays on the unity of God, on happiness, and on resurrection, and a defense of Jews who make apparent conversion under duress.

The Medical Writings

The complete medical works of Maimonides include ten comprehensive books according to various calculations.* His own basic knowledge of medicine derived from studies of Arabic writers who had themselves been strongly grounded in the works of Galen. He himself wrote an interpretation of Galenic medicine which became widely known as the Medical Principles of the Aphorisms of Maimonides. This contains emphasis on some of the contradictions in Galen as well as criticisms of Galenic medicine and philosophy. He wrote also a commentary on the Hippocratic Aphorisms derived from Galen's exposition of these aphorisms.

* 1) Book on Asthma 2) Poisons and their Antidotes 3) Guide to Good Health 4) Aphorisms of Moses 5) On Cohabitation 6) Commentary to the Treatises of Hippocrates 7) On Hemorrhoids 8) Medical Responsa 9) The Names of Drugs 10) A Compendium of the Treatises of Galen.

According to George Sarton, next in popularity to the aphorisms was a work written in 1198 for Saladin's eldest son. Maimonides fame as a physician brought him the patronage of the vizier of Saladin who recommended him to the court. The son of Saladin suffered from attacks of depression. For him Maimonides wrote what would be considered today a book of health for the layman. Maimonides explains the case and gives rules for healthful living following the precepts of Hippocrates and Galen; he suggests home remedies for use when traveling away from contact with the physician. Next comes some practical pyschotherapy for Maimonides recognized the influence of mind on body and vice versa, which we now call psychosomatic medicine. This book ends with aphorisms on hygiene and dietetics.

Other works of Maimonides deal with accidents, poisons and their antidotes, hemorrhoids, sexual intercourse and a pharmacopeia of the period.

The book on asthma was written for a nephew of Saladin; Sarton says it was written about 1190 for an unknown patient in Alexandria. Dr. Salo Wittmayer Baron asserts simply that it was written for a patient of high rank. Sarton writes that this work was translated into Latin by Armengaud in 1302 and into Hebrew (from the Latin) by the Spanish Jew Samuel ben Benveniste about 1320. Another Hebrew translation was made from the Arabic by Joshua Shatibi (of Xativa) about the end of the 14th century. To this Baron adds that a Hebrew translation was published by Suessman Muntner as Vol. 1 of Maimonides' Ketubim refuiim in Jerusalem in 1940. This should probably be Dr. Süssmann Muntner under whose leadership the translation into English here published has been prepared.

According to Professor Baron the treatise begins with

an introduction in which Maimonides relates the complaints of the patient. These include what are called "stenocardiac symptoms" and such violent headache that the patient could not wear a turban. The patient himself inquired whether he had not better have a change of air and transfer his residence from Alexandria to Cairo. Maimonides explains first the general rules regarding diet and suitable climatic conditions. Then he discusses the special diet suitable for sufferers from asthma. Then follow a number of recipes and a review of the ailments and climates of different countries of the near East. The healthiness of the dry Egyptian climate for asthmatics is emphasized. However, he adds that one can bring the condition to an end in Egypt by diet alone without the use of remedies. Maimonides emphasizes that the use of strong remedies is dangerous and he refers to the case of the Morocan Emir who dies in 1142 because he took too strong a dose of theriac prescribed by his doctors.

When one considers the reasoning powers and the accomplishments of Maimonides in the light of the times in which he lived admiration is boundless. Reared in a hostile atmosphere, compelled to simulate a belief in religion against every principle which had been inculcated in him, fleeing before the constant threat of persecution, his scientific mind nevertheless raised questions for which he sought answers.

The true scientist has always been subject to attack by the superstitious and the credulous who are obviously in the majority and who dislike to see their beliefs destroyed. Maimonides exposed the contradictions of the Galenic writings. He wrote a letter to the rabbis of Marseilles in which he condemned astrology as a system of superstitions. According to Sarton, he made the first complete classification and codification of all the Mosaic and rabbinical laws. In this he tried to simplify the subject and codify the vast and complex Talmudic law. His writings which laid great emphasis on the rationale raised bitter opposition. For a hundred years camps existed of those for and against the views of Maimonides. The enmity between the two parties became so great that the dispute was referred in 1234 to the papal legate at Montpellier, who ordered Maimonides' works to be destroyed. There were public burnings of the writings of Maimonides. Consider the folly of burning books! On many occasions, the latest being in the period of Hitler, books have been publicly burned, only to give in most instances, far more importance to what was burned, than it might otherwise have had. More than eight hundred years after the birth of Maimonides his words and his thoughts are studied in the colleges and universities, translated into the languages of many peoples, read and reread for ideas and meanings that might have been overlooked. Many of his manuscripts are existing in most of European National libraries so also in the library of the Vatican, through the cordial cooperation of Pope Pius have been made available in photostatic copies to the Israel Torah Research Institute and to Professor Süssman Muntner for translation and commentary.

Various bibliographies of the writings of Maimonides, of comments and criticisms, and of historical reviews have been published in many languages. Many scholars have made careers of such studies. Many items have been credited to him, as to Hippocrates, for which he had scant if any responsibility. The prayer for the physician which has been published and republished was probably written long after Maimonides had died. Whoever the writer of the prayer, he caught something of the dignity and the respect held by Maimonides for those devoted to the care and healing of the sick.

In an intimate letter by Maimonides at the height of

his career in Egypt, he tells something of his daily life. The demands on his time by royalty forced him to go early in the morning to the palace to attend the sultan, the relatives, and all the retinue. This occupied him until late in the afternoon. Then he returned home and in his weariness he threw himself on a couch and from this position still saw patients and others who came to seek his advice. At this time he took some nourishment which was his only meal of the day. As an orthodox observing Jew, he found it impossible to partake of food served in the palace. He reflects that so little time was left for him to care for the needy. Yet his attainments were so revered that sick people, from among the poorest Jews of Cairo were carried, until recent years, to the synagogue of Maimonides to spend the night in an underground chamber. Sarton suggests that this is a survival of the Egyptian and Greek rite of a similar character.

In Tiberias in Israel one may see the tomb of Maimonides. Legend has it that the body was being carried on the back of a donkey and fell off at the point where it is buried. Many thousands of people visit the tomb each year to give respect to the memory of this great man. He was a pious orthodox Jew and an ardent scientist in observing, recording and analysing the phenomena of nature. He saw in Nature the existence of a rational God. Says Sarton: "In common with every other philosopher who was more inclined to rationalism than to mysticism, he emphasized the ethical side of religion; man must be good before he can be wise."

Chicago, January, 1963

Editor's Note

The present book *On Asthma* (in Hebrew 'Sefer Haqazereth' or "Sefer Hamis'adim") is the first of a series of ten medical books by the great Maimonides to appear in the English language. It was also the first of Maimonides' medical works to have been published by the present editor in an annotated Hebrew edition with a running commentary on linguistic, medical and historical points, as far back as 1940.

Despite the exciting nature of its contents from the medical, historical and autobiographical points of view neither the Arabic original nor its early Hebrew and Latin versions have so far seen the light of day. Admittedly, there was little in the crude early translations to make them appeal to the public taste.

The first Hebrew edition of the book *On Asthma* was followed by similar editions of Maimonides' *Poisons and their Antidotes*, *Regimen Sanitatis* (for bodily and mental health), *Medical Aphorisms of Maimonides*, and the *Commentary to the Aphorisms of Hippocrates*, with his remaining works kept ready for publication. Critical editions of some other books have been published only in the last few decades, by H. Kroner and Max Meyerhof.

I am grateful to the ITRI FOUNDATION for bringing the present English edition into being. I was further encouraged and assisted by the kind endeavors of Dr. Béla Schick and Dr. M. Murray Peshkin, of New York, as well as by the devoted enterprise of Dr. Morris Fishbein, for many years the distinguished editor of the *Journal of the American Medical Association*.

In preparing the English translation, which is based on my annotated Hebrew edition and reinforced by constant references to the Arabic and Latin MSS., I was assisted by Dr. M. Rosen and Dr. Kopf. Walter Kahoe, Director of the Medical Publications Division of the Lippincott Company, was kind enough to supervise and correct the English text.

To all who have assisted and cooperated with me in this project many thanks are due from me as well as from the 750 years old genius of Moses Maimonides, who is here presented for the first time to the scientific and medical public in a modern and universal language.

I have five other medical works by Maimonides ready for publication and intend them to follow one another in quick succession, the others will follow after their first edition in Hebrew which is going on.

Words or sentences occurring in parentheses in this edition are the Editor's addition to the original text, and are designed to offer a better understanding of its contents.

Jerusalem,   S. MUNTNER, M.D.
January, 1963

Treatise on Asthma

ON ASTHMA

Said the Rabbi, Rabbenu Moshe ben Maimon Abdallah of Cordova, the Israelite:

His Highness the Prince, our Benefactor (may God keep him in good health for many years to come) has consulted me about the grave disease that befell him, which in other languages is called RINAPLI (Asthma) and in Arabic ALRABU. He graciously asked me to lay down for him the dietary measures he should either avoid or adopt as well as the general rules of conduct which might be useful in this illness.

Elsewhere we have already pointed out the fact, known to great medical teachers of former times, as well as to the physicians of our day, that this disease has many etiological aspects and should be treated according to the various causes that bring it about. Physicians are well aware that this disease cannot be managed successfully without a full knowledge of the patient's constitution as a whole and of his individual organs, especially that of the ailing part and its companions in pain.

Furthermore we must consider whether the patient is fat or lean, which is also part of his bodily constitution. Then should be considered his age and habits as well as the season of the year. I intended to deal with the problem at large, i.e., to describe all the circumstances under which this illness may appear—the times, the places and causes thereof—it would take me too far afield since all these questions should be dealt with

I

separately. Such is not the intention of the present book, since all these have already been discussed by various medical authors. The symptoms of this disease are common knowledge and its causes too well known to warrant a special treatise on my part. Furthermore, I have *no magic cure* to report and all I have in mind in writing this book is to meet the wishes of His Highness —may God bestow good health upon him (to describe a certain diethetic regimen).

From what I have heard from others, and as is known to Your Highness,[1] I conclude that this disorder[2] starts with a common cold, especially in the rainy season, and the patient is forced to gasp for breath day and night, depending on the duration of the onset, until the phlegm is expelled, the flow completed and the lung well cleared. This is all I know about the prodromal phases of this illness. You have also told me you were in the habit of taking once or twice a year certain remedies to clear the nose and the lung and often, when resorted to during an attack, these tend to weaken you. I also know that you are about forty years of age, your body build moderate (neither fat nor lean), your bodily vigour about average, that you are rather hot-blooded and your head liable to become easily inflamed. You also remarked that strong winds tend to hurt you and sharp smells offend you much. Hair weighs on you heavily and repeated shaving of the head brings you some comfort. You wear no headdress and no turban, all of which goes to show that your head suffers from excessive heat. Your Highness has already confided in me that the air of Alexandria is harmful to you and whenever you fear an attack of the illness you prefer to move to Cairo where the air is much dryer and calmer, making the attack more tolerable for you. You also told me that many physicians prescribed for you remedies of all kinds, each one of them proclaiming his cure to be the best, but that none of them cured your disorder.

Having set out what a physician is expected to consider before he embarks upon the treatment of his patient I ask your Highness' forgiveness lest I happen to give advice already tendered elsewhere. With this I come to make reply to Your Highness' request of me.

In this treatise I intend to include general articles which might be of use to all people as to the preservation of their health and the prevention and cure of many diseases. In writing them down I followed the advice of Galen and other physicians inasmuch as I remember it. Furthermore, I shall cite the names of the sources I relied upon, to lend greater force to my discourse.

At the end of the book I intend to give advice of a general nature which might be useful in teaching how to keep in good health, generally and how to go about treating specific cases in particular. *My intention is to serve humanity as a whole, so that Your Highness as well as the rest of mankind may profit by it.*

I thought it best to divide this treatise into several chapters, so that the reader may remember it well and also find, with the help of God, the subject he is looking for without undue loss of time:

CHAPTER ONE advises on the best course of personal conduct in general.

CHAPTER TWO treats of the dietary measures which should be adopted or avoided when afflicted with the disease under consideration.

CHAPTER THREE treats of the foods to be taken or eschewed, with special emphasis on the foods of familiar origin.

At the beginning of each Chapter I also give a preview of its contents. May God assist me in this labor.

I

Which Treats of the Best Course of General Conduct (Dietetic) Which All Who Read This Book Should Know

1. IN ALL grave disorders marked by seizures, such as lumbago, inflammation of the joints, gravel (in the kidney), asthma (also called shortness of breath), migraine, also called the half-head sickness, and the like and other diseases wholly or partly incurable—in all of them, provided the prescribed regimen is well kept and judiciously applied, the intervals between two onsets may be lengthened, the duration of the onset shortened and its intensity mitigated. However, should the rules of management go unheeded and one's desires and habits be followed indiscriminately, the gap between onsets will grow shorter, and the duration and intensity gradually increase until a peak is reached which may well end in death.

Even when one of the bodily organs is weak from birth and suffering from a regular intake of diseased humours, even then might a well-observed regime soften the humours and thereby ease the patient's condition. On the other hand, a haphazard diet will cause the (bad) humours to multiply and the attacks to grow worse.

On this point, which is of great importance in all branches of medicine, Galen has already remarked as follows: A striking proof of what we said before is the

5

man in whose sick organs the cough appears once in six months or at greater intervals and then, when his whole body is weakened, the sickness becomes a regular (chronic) condition. This shows that the cause of the illness is not always known and that there is at work another factor stirring up the embers of the disease which becomes protracted and worse.

2. Says the Author: Galen already explained and illustrated the fact that the weakened organs succumb to disease because of excessive humours even when they are good humours and also because of the bad humours even when they are small in number. The more humours there are and the worse their kind the greater the damage. Galen also emphasizes the fact that he cured many people who kept, for years, a prescribed diet and behaved as they were told. Furthermore, Galen says that the damage extends also to moral qualities, because of bad drinking and eating habits. On the other hand, a purposeful diet improves the spiritual powers mightily. These regulations should be observed and followed to good advantage both in illness and in good health.

3. It is well known that the course of dietary conduct for the healthy and sick alike has been grouped by the physicians in seven categories, of which six are obligatory and unconditional and the seventh commendable. The six obligatory regulations are: (1) keeping clean the air which we breathe; (2) keeping an eating and drinking diet; (3) regulation of spiritual emotions, (4) regulation of bodily exercise, and lastly, rest, (5) sleep and waking up, (6) excretion, eventually keeping back of superfluous outflow. The seventh group is the one the body takes according to circumstance, such as bathing and massaging.

6

Maimonides
Rabenu Moshe Ben Maimon (1135–1204)

The ancient Hebrew translation of "Asthma" by R. Shmuel Benbenisti (XIII Cent.) of Saragossa. (Cod. Hebr. Paris, 1173)

No physician of antiquity included in his general health regime the regulation of coitus. However, Hippocrates mentions it in his diet for sick people when it becomes important, in the case of some bad constitutions, to conserve the semen outflow. But in most cases people indulge in it without any cause, other than from lust. To my mind regulation of coitus should be included in this seventh group.

4. In the following chapters I shall deal in detail with each of the seven groups and mention it when the occasion calls for it.

II

Which Discusses the Kinds of Food Which Should be Taken or Avoided in This Disease

1. FAT AND COARSE FOOD[3] should be avoided as far as possible. Furthermore avoid a too rich meal, even if it tastes well. Any food containing much residue should be avoided at all cost. It is well to take food in moderate quantities, even less than usual, and even the small amount consumed should be not too condensed or rough. The reason therefor is quite clear: in digestion the less fat and coarse foods leave behind a certain amount of unassimilated parts which escape the body in the form of gases and sweat. If more residue is left behind (from the less fatty foods) it easily escapes the body through the pores of the skin, in the stool and urine or in other channels of excretion. Should however the residue be too solid or rough its dissolution is beset with difficulties and its exit from the body outlets greatly hampered. It then wanders about from organ to organ and hinders evacuation. If the digestive organs are strongly resistant to the residue the latter moves to less resistant organs where they settle down and aggravate their weaknesses. A physician wishing to soften and dislodge it must have recourse to strong emetics or spend a long time on it, or both, all depending upon the degree of fattiness and coarseness or the number of pathogenic juices, and also on the narrowness and length of the evacuation tract, and the

8

weakness and strength of the organs and their surroundings. This is explained by the fact that some (pathogenic) juices are rather obstinate and not easily affected by the doctor's wishes and do not budge once they have settled down. Gradually they destroy everything that stands in their way thus leading to severe disease and to the loss of some organ or of the entire body. A fattening diet is therefore offensive conduct in any man. It may even endanger life since the object is not to overload the vessels but to keep the pores open and the evacuation tract absolutely cleared so as to prevent any obstruction and contraction and so to enable superfluous gases and juices to leave easily.

In one of his sayings Galen speaks of the diligence and care to be exercised to have the openings of the digestive organs and the channels from the liver cleared and clean at all times, not only in the sick but in the healthy as well. In another passage he says as follows: This is why I advise all people to eschew all foods tending to generate bad juices. Also people with a rapid and easy digestion should not expose themselves to the danger of a false diet because in time the bad juices concentrate in the blood vessels which do not turn the bad juices to gases. Add to this the smallest cause leading to rot and you have ulcers and high temperature.

2. Says the Author: It is a most useful thing and valuable counsel for every man to beware of fat food in general. But where this disease (asthma) is concerned, and the man here discussed in particular, a fattening diet is destructive to the body whereas a delicate fare is highly commendable. However, one should not fall into either extreme, and a middling course between obesity and leanness is advisable. Next it is important to keep away from all food which generates gas and mounts to the head. This is especially the case

9

when the food is scalding hot, because the weakness of the head[4] is aggravated by additional heat, and such (additional) heat is, it seems, the cause of Your Highness' indisposition. Galen has already pointed out that all body organs fail to exercise their power when unhinged from their central course and leaning much in one direction or another. Further (he said) any heated organ tends to attract residue so that most of the residue concentrates not in the brain but in the lungs which become heated, as is the case in this disease. The bronchioli and the alveoli, ramifying from the bronchi, fill with phlegm and become immersed in it. It transpires, therefore, that all food difficult to digest should be avoided since all food hard on the stomach remains there for a long time and some of the gases mount to the brain where they cause pressure, swelling the brain, and weakening it. This is what I have found to be useful for Your Highness in this chapter of the present book.

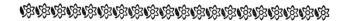

III

Which Treats of the Foods Which Should be Avoided or Made Use of, with Special Reference to Popular Local Foods

1. GALEN HAS already told us that anything prepared from grossly sifted wheat flour generates fat, phlegm and is hard on digestion but is otherwise very nourishing. The injurious effect remains unless the flour is finely ground and enriched with leaven and salt, the dough well kneaded and notched and well baked in the oven. Bread so prepared is better than that produced from whole grain and is well digested in the stomach. Next in importance to the bread baked in the oven comes the furnace bread; next to the fine flour comes flour produced from wheat which has not been soaked and shelled in water but subjected to a medium sifting so as not to lose all the bran and finally halfground. Such flour when kneaded and baked in the aforesaid manner is a nutritious, wholesome and appetizing food, easily digested and moderately satisfying. Anything else prepared otherwise from wheat is damaging to all people and to Your Highness in particular. Therefore I need not give special warning against dishes based on wheat, such as mortar-pounded semolina and the more or less cleft wheat barley, or against cooked dishes based on flour such as flour pudding, neither against paste products such as

noodles, what people call Elitrya (macaroni), spaghetti, etc., nor against those mixed with or fried in oil because these increase phlegm and cause heat, as do pastries made with fat, flat cakes, and pancakes. Most damaging are also puff-paste products because they are un-leavened, sticky and half baked. When in addition to this they are also treated with cane sugar, dipped in honey and fried, they are the cause of diseases which even healthy people fall prey to, and much more sick people who should improve their juices and reject from their food any sticky substances. All flour dishes which act as fattening agents increase as a rule the sticky juices, as we have noted before. Should they in addition be treated with honey or cane-sugar they become greatly harmful to the liver which they tend to obstruct; and, because their flavor moves to the liver whereby it absorbs much gall and finally spreads through the whole liver and moves from there to the veins to block them as well. This Your Highness should know and take more active steps to avoid these and all other things cautioned against. From all this Your Highness will understand that the flour should be finely ground, pro-duced from the innermost grain of wheat and innocent of any admixture.

2. Says Galen: Anything produced from wheat gener-ates thick juices which move about with difficulty. They block the vessels which carry nourishment to the organs, the spleen is dammed up and becomes dis-tended, gravel is formed in the kidneys.

3. To this point speaks the Author: Moreover, one should avoid all flatulent seed such as black beans (Vicia faba), peas, haricot beans, chickpeas, also all obstructive seed such as rice and lentils or such that fill the head with gases such as nuts and such that

increase heat such as leek (Allium porrum), onion and garlic. Further one should avoid heavy meats such as beef, and goat's meat and mutton which Galen insists are even heavier than beef.

4. It is well known that cheese is regarded as a thick-juiced food and is especially harmful when very old. All the kinds of milk usually consumed bring about a stuffing in the head and Your Highness would do best to keep away from them. Also fowls living on the water, such as goose and duck which contain many harmful juices, are thick juiced and hard on digestion. Your Highness is advised to choose chicken meat that is not fat, i.e., contains little residue and is easily digested, likewise the hazel-hen (durag'), the turtle-dove and the capercaillie. The smaller the fowl, such as tiny birds, the more useful they are in this disease, especially when roasted or prepared in the pan with gruel. The soup of fat hens is an effective remedy in this disease, yolk of hens' eggs, otherwise an excellent food, especially when half-boiled, is advisedly not to be too much indulged in because of the many juices it produces. Deep-sea fish, being slenderly built, poor in fat, tasteful and easily cooked, containing little sticky substance (mucus) and little residue, are good food for Your Highness. River fish, too, are recommended provided they come from big streams of pure water.

5. So far I have spoken of the scaly fish which suit this disease. Widely recommended for this ailment is the salty fish because of its delicacy and tender flesh. However my advice is not to consume it too often because it toughens up the phlegm. I also advise eating the kind of fish called "muglas" as well as the smoothly cleft kind, containing little salt. But this is of use only when taken not more than once or twice in the month.

6. Always prefer the meat of young sheep which is, being the general preference and easily procured, also of much help. It is well to take a yearling or a sheep starting its second year of life; let Your Highness not use one that already completed its second year. Only sheep from the open pasture should be taken, not stable-fed, because they contain much offal (residue), especially the fat ones. The flesh of the female of this small cattle is rather harmful for all people and especially Your Highness, because of its thick mucus, toughness and rich residue.

Their haunches though, contain no (superfluous) juices but abound in thick mucus. Even from the male animal Your Highness would do well to use as a rule only the meat of the front part, i.e., the shoulder and ribmeat above the heart. Your Highness should at all times beware of the intestinal fat which is absolutely harmful for all people because of its thick mucus and damage to digestion. It satisfies easily and stops the appetite. When taken in this illness it corrupts all the organs to which it carries its juices. Never should food contain much fat, even in (useful) meat as explained above. Should it contain much fat then the fat should be removed and no more left on the meat than what is required for its tasteful preparation.

7. Know that the meat of roe, ram and hare is excellent for this complaint, although the nutritional value of these foods is not outstanding. Similarly praised in this regard is the fat of the hare. However, exceeding everything in curative value in this disease, even if its nutritional value is very small, is fox meat, especially lung; likewise the meat of the wild hedgehog is exceptionally useful in this disease because it dries up the harmful substances (in the body) and restores order

where this could be done. The useful part is its lung, especially in this illness.

8. Of vegetables the following are highly recommended in this disease: beetroot, asparagus, even if it is hard on digestion, fennel, parsley, mint, pennyroyal (Mentha pulegium), summer savory (origanum), water-cresses, radish (Raphanus sativus). All these, even if their nutritional value is slight, act against this complaint. Vegetables of cooling nature and remedies containing much moisture such as lettuce, garden orache (Armoles hortensis), mallow (Moluchia), pumpkin (Coloquinte) etc., are definitely harmful in this disease and should be altogether avoided.

The same applies to fleshy plants such as taro (colocassia, Arum colocassia), Swedish turnip (Brassica napus), pastinaca agrestis, cauliflower (Brassica oleracea), eggplant (Solanum melongena), turnip (Brassica rapa). All these should best be avoided by Your Highness because of their fleshiness, even if their juices do have a softening effect. Your Highness must not consume them in any form whatever since they accumulate injurious and thickening substances.

9. Fruit rich in moisture, such as watermelon, peaches, apricots, mulberries (morus), cucumber (Cucumis sativus), and gherkin, is bad because all such fruit is considered bad for people generally, especially when speaking of those here concerned and particularly so in this illness. Here belong also fresh dates in half ripe condition. These should be eaten when juicy and full of substance, otherwise they give rise to headaches. Also grapes, which cause flatulence. All blossoming things, say the doctors, fill the head with gases and greatly hamper digestion. However, if some juice is

15

taken in the morning on an empty stomach and followed up with a dish of a pronounced sour taste such as menthe there is, I believe, no harm in it. Fresh figs, on the other hand, are allowed but should not be taken continually; although also being flatulent they have the advantage of rapidly leaving the stomach thus causing hardly any damage. Like other fruit they are best consumed on an empty stomach. However, once they are peeled, ripe fruits may be enjoyed at will. When taken together with porridge, vinegar or salt, peganum (Ruta graveolens) pennyroyal (mint) and cumin (Cuminum cyminum), they act as medicine, liquifying and purging. If it pleases Your Highness to partake of one of these foods it is best to have some after you have finished with the figs. On the day the figs leave your stomach you should take a light meal such as young chicken or turtle dove or small fowl seasoned with vinegar and lemon juice and cooked in menthe (mint, pennyroyal). Should Your Highness follow it up with pomegranate juice your chest would feel much better.[5]

10. Sucking of quince after meals is recommended but should not be indulged to excess. All preserved stodgy fruit such as quince, the fruit of zizyphus spina-Christi (nabaq) and of hemlock (crataegus azarolus) are injurious to sick people of this kind. Apple, too, is injurious because of its stodginess and flatulency. Raisins assist digestion, soften the stool and mitigate the burn in the anus, stomach and respiratory channel, but their stones should be discarded. The same applies to dried figs which may be consumed after dipping them in the juice of grated and strained dill. Your Highness may always complete your meals with pistachio nuts and almonds, especially the bitter kind mixed with the sweet, until it becomes a habit with

you, since they are a perfect remedy for this illness, liquifying the bodily juices, clearing all the obstructions in the bronchi and contributing to clear thinking. A similar effect is produced by the big cinnabar fruits of pinus pinea. They purge the lungs, especially when soaked in warm water. They become edible after the water dries up. There is no harm in hazelnuts when taken in small quantities but walnuts should be shunned because they generate gases which mount to the brain (head). It is well to consume the stones of all these fruits well dried and sweetened with sugar or other sweetening substances but unmixed with any wheat grain or sesame kernels.

﷽﷽﷽﷽﷽﷽﷽﷽﷽﷽﷽﷽﷽﷽﷽﷽﷽

IV

Which Treats of Recipes for the Preparation of Dishes
Useful in This Disease

1. I HAVE ALREADY described the nature of foods which
should be avoided in this disease. I have up to now
mentioned their properties insofar as they are used
separately. Now after this we can treat of dishes made
up from the foods we know and which are in general
use[6] namely, peganum (Ruta graveolens), melongena
(badingan), beet (also Lactica sativa), chicken or
mutton, as we suggested to Your Highness before.
Such a dish if cooked with beans, (should Your Highness not care for beans) its soup is still good for your
health.

2. To these dishes belong also the shumkaya[7] which is
of the greatest use, tasting superb and having curative
value, too. This is prepared as follows: cook mutton or
chicken, then grill it the way other comestibles are
done, as explained hereafter; then take the grilled meat
out and put it aside, next raisins with pips removed
are soaked in vinegar for two hours. Then the raisins
are crushed in a mortar with one fourth shelled almonds and the matter forced through a sieve so that
the skins of the raisins disappear too. All this is poured
onto the roasted meat until it is perfectly done. I have
seen this dish in Egypt and greatly approved of its

combination because it helps digestion, warms moderately, tends to keep the body dry and opens up the pores. It suits all healthy people, and particularly benefits the sick we are here concerned with.

3. The advantage of this combination lies in the fact that the raisins supply the liver with important food elements and greatly benefit it thereby, that they do away with heartburn, clear the lungs and lend the body quiet and comfort. Some people say that when taken excessively it burns up the blood. The vinegar acts as a disrupting and liquifying factor, clearing all obstructions but is harmful to the liver which it irritates, creates white gall in the blood, affects the air channels by drying them up, generates thick phlegm which renders coughing difficult. However when mixed up each part mollifies the bad effect of the others and only the useful parts remain, especially when mixed in chicken soup or with almond kernels. I don't believe I have ever come across a better combination than this.

4. Then, matsuts soup (in which the meat is cooked in vinegar) with but little vinegar used, and the zirbag soup (bouillon, broth) is recommended. No less useful is (the soup) prepared with sugar, almonds or saffron (qirtami or wild saffron, called mamerzig). Next, almonds[8] done in rose-leaf preserves and kept over the winter are highly recommended and should be consumed at all times. Likewise the dish prepared from honey with froth skimmed, or with sugar, some vinegar and lemonade and finally seasoned with spikenard[9] is a useful combination. For the winter season a dish prepared from fennel greens is recommended. The green leaves are cooked, then the inner part removed and cooked again. When the cooking is over a lean hen is put in with chicken soup poured over it smothered in

leaves and grilled. By grilling (roasting) we mean that no water is added in the pot during the process excepting the fluid that strains from the meat while it is being cooked. All this is left on the fire until well done. Shoots of fennel, grown and peeled, crushed to spice and cooked together with the above-mentioned dish, is excellent food serving to soften the stool. This food is well known in our Western parts, highly popular and useful. When there is added to the mamerzig soup in the process of cooking one fourth of this, and also porridge and some mild seasoning and the soup left on the fire until done, it becomes exceedingly tasteful and easily digestible.

5. A staple food with the Egyptians is salted bread, with vinegar and skimmed honey, or with vinegar and honey, or vinegar and sugar, or with gruel. This is always to be found on their tables especially in winter.

6. They dip bits of bread in the juice of the kind of onion called hog's onion and sometimes also in mustard. With us in Spain the mustard mayonnaise is prepared as follows: one measure (*ca.* 1 kg.) of Damascus mustard (Sinapis syriaca) is soaked throughout the night in warm water, after which the water is poured off. Then the mustard is put in a stone mortar with some clean wadding to keep it in place, so that it does not rise in the air when pounded; strong vinegar is added and everything finely ground. Then some good olive oil is gradually added until the one measure (qaw) absorbs a full liter of oil, with vinegar being stirred into it. Then a pound of sweet peeled almonds are ground until they look like marrow and then sifted through linen cloth or sieve until milky in appearance and indistinguishable from milk except by taste. This very much assists digestion, does away with phlegm,

liquifies stomach contents and softens the strong juices without having too strong a warming effect on the body.

7. Know that warming up and drying agents (foods and remedies) are particularly harmful in this sickness, above all in a constitution such as that of Your Highness, because they thicken up the food-carrying juices and cause the lean organs to fuse together in growth and to stiffen. This is why I see to it (in everything I prescribe for you) that in your food no flavor is found of spices which are of a pronounced warming quality, and are widely popular in this part of the world. To avoid such bad effects the above combination should be mixed with half an ounce of green pepper, two ounces each of cabbage stalks[10], garden cabbage, cauliflower (Brassica oleracea), half an ounce of ginger, 3 zuzim (ca. 5 grams) of spikenard (Nardostachys), 2 zuzim (ca. 3.5 grams) of masish,[11] (Pistacia lentiscus), and six zuzim of coriander (gad, kuzbar). All this is crushed and the dish seasoned with it so that the body does not experience any warming up. On the other hand there is no harm even in dishes prepared in vinegar, mentioned above, if they are treated with ginger (zerumbet-zarunbad), blossoms of aromatic cloves and the cedar[12] (folia pini cedri), 2 zuzim of each (ca. 3.5 grams); they even help evacuation by softening and melting down stomach contents in spite of the vinegar. Anything else added to the food is local custom and should not be left out because these ingredients contribute to digestion, soften the stool and warm up the body no more than necessary.

8. However, all farinaceous foods in which pure wheat flour[13] occurs are bad, even those which contain only a modicum of wheat such as chawitza (sorbitio), ome-

lette with dates, fat and amylum, or karia fritters (wheat paste stuffed with meat) which in Egypt pass off as pastry, and many others. All these are digested with difficulty and cause constipation.[14] I have already discussed before the advisability of using dried sweet food in the chapter dealing with fruits, also the fruit of the stone-pine coated with fanid (a mixture of cane sugar and sweet almonds), as they coat the pistachio nut or dip it into it.

Arabic original written in Hebrew characters, by R. Abraham Maimonides, the son of Moses Maimonides. (Cod. Hebr. Paris, 1211)

Latin manuscript, translated from original Arabic and Hebrew by Joannes di Capua (XIV Cent.) at the request of a contemporary pope suffering from asthma. (Cod. Latin Friedenwald-Jerusalem)

V

Which Treats of the Quantity of Food to be Taken

1. HAVING SPOKEN so far of the nature of foods it is time we embark on a discourse on quantities. This is naturally bound up with individual differences, which means that some who boast a big stomach and a robust digestion can absorb a bigger intake of food while others who have a small stomach and a weak digestion can cope only with small amounts of food. Medical art (regarding dosage) is also known to follow this principle.[14a] It is good for any man to know his normal measure of food when healthy. He can base his estimate on what he can stand easily in springtime and on what affects his digestion favorably. This amount should serve him as a norm to which to refer. The hotter the day the less food should he take, the colder the day the more food should he gradually add to his diet. The main thing is to beware of surfeit which leads to the distension of the belly beyond normal measure. For any member in a state of tension fails to function properly since all swelling is a separation of adjoining parts. When the stomach reaches beyond its natural size its functioning power declines because it stops forwarding the food that has entered it. This gives rise to a feeling of heaviness and satiety (nausea) resulting in a craving for liquids without being actually thirsty, merely to neutralize the food[15] and to alleviate the sense of oppression by immersion in fluids. This

ies behind the excessive lust for beverages after a heavy meal.

2. Doctors have laid down the following rule: That a man should stop eating before he experiences a sense of repletion (nausea), that is, as soon as he satisfies his appetite; even if he stays just hungry (after finishing his meal). If an animal, meaning a horse, donkey and camel to which no self-limiting (rules) were taught, can take the exact measure of its fullness and not overstep it, how can a man fail to know his proper food intake, and take more food than he can possibly cram into himself until it sticks in his throat (until it reaches his gullet)?

3. I have seen gluttons who throw their food and poke it back into their mouths like ruminating beasts. This is one of the biggest causes of many diseases. A rich meal, even consisting of the choicest dishes, when exaggerated leads directly to the loss of digestive power. Thereby bad juices are generated which are the chief cause of the worst diseases. Galen has pointed out the fact that they can cause death within one day, or in some cases after two or three days, or can lead to chronic illness. Surfeit causes also heartburn, diarrhea, pain in the pit of the stomach, finally fainting fits (also angina pectoris). This chapter is not intended to suggest remedies for the various stomach ills but it does aim at eliminating them beforehand and showing up their extreme peril and so prevent them altogether.

4. Doctors advise against consuming a great number of dishes at a single meal. They say one dish is enough. The reason therefore lies in the varying degree of digestibility (of the different foods). There is only one stomach. When different kinds of dishes go into it juices are naturally formed which affect digestion in a

24

more or less different way. Best digested is a single, uncombined dish. Also, doctors believe that a great deal of harm is caused by the wrong order in which dishes are served, which must be avoided. Foods, it appears, can lose their digestibility for several reasons: (1) because of (bad) quality, (2) because of excessive amount, as explained above, and (3) also because of their wrong succession on the table. Some say it is important to eat first the heavy and then light dishes. Galen thinks the light dishes should come first. Others are of the opinion that first one should eat the foods which make for a "loose stomach" and then astringents. Should however both kinds be taken in a single pot dish there is no need to watch the serving order mentioned above. This latter dish, I believe, is more advisable than the other two because diverse dishes sharpen the appetite which increases with every one of them. On the other hand, the single pot dish lessens the appetite and one should never take from it more than necessary. Only an exceptionally big glutton can overeat himself on such a dish. However, a single dish is admittedly less substantial than a full-course dinner. A sound diet requires the least (possible) number of courses and (even in these) a man should stop short of repletion.

5. Says Hippocrates: Good health depends on avoidance of overeating and sinking in idleness and indolence. Galen, too, cites a most useful precept in this regard which I repeat here because I think it very important. It reads like this: inactivity is as big an evil where preservation of good health is aimed at as moderate exercise is a great boon to it. This means that a man would not become ill (so easily) were he assured of a good digestion all the time. This is why he should refrain from making any physical exertion soon after

meals. The reason therefor is this: just as there is nothing more useful for the preservation of health than physical exercise before meals so there is nothing more harmful than (excessive) exercise soon after meals. This is because in the latter case the food leaves the stomach (prematurely) and spreads all over the body before it is (fully) digested. This results in a massive accumulation of bad juices in the veins which bring about all kinds of diseases unless they are dissolved by strenuous work or assimilated in the blood through the agency of the liver and arteries.

6. Says the Author: There is great profit in resting after meals. Consequently, the taking of a (steam) bath, coitus and bloodletting immediately after eating is a major offense (against good health), because all entail (strenuous) exercise. The only proper thing to do after meals is resting. One should always keep in mind the advantages of safeguarding against bad digestion which is the undisputed cause of stomach complaints (nausea, vomiting, heartburn). Galen indeed enumerates a number of cases, saying as follows: All these are apparently examples of people who do not digest their food (well enough). In one man one symptom of the disease may appear, in another several of them, all depending upon the differences in body build, age, disposition (susceptibility) and upon the diversity of harmful foods. The symptoms appearing upon insufficient and bad digestion are as follows: a sense of repletion (gases), heartburn, loose stool or frequent diarrhea, impotence, loss of appetite, insomnia, stomach ache, giddiness or mental aberration, lethargy, eventually mental depression, etc., colic (i.e., pains in the belly) or retention of urine, or inflammation of the kidneys, of the spleen, liver, joints or general discomfort, or ague with shivers or temperature.

7. Says the Author: It is fitting that the healthy intelligent man should well reconsider the point whether the appetizing dish before him is well worth the risk. Galen spoke about and arrived at the conclusion that the only way out is to consume a single hearty dish, not too much of it and no active exercise soon after it, as emphasized above. If this preventive measure is made obligatory with regard to the healthy how much more important is it for the sick who actually suffer from all these maladies, and in particular for those whose vital organs are weak by nature and, generally, in all diseases in which a set diet (regimen) is required. (For all these) it is very important that they keep the rules with regard to the use of foods and their quantities in the manner explained above.

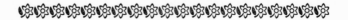

VI

Which Treats of the Time Meals Should be Taken

1. IN THIS RESPECT customs vary. Most eat in the morning and evening, others eat thrice a day, some once a day. I do not know how Your Highness conducts himself in this regard. The general rule to be followed is for healthy, vigorous people to consume all the nourishment they need at one sitting a day. On the other hand, if debilitated persons, such as old men and convalescents, take their daily meal all at once they commit an outrage against their health. They must portion it out according to the degree of their debility so that their powers do not fail them altogether and their native warmth depart.

2. Of the rule of diet for old people says Galen as follows: The main rule to be adhered to is that a person of limited physical strength should be given small meals within short intervals and one of full bodily vigor—a single meal at long intervals.

3. To this says the Author: this precept recurs ever again in his books and what it practically amounts to is that one should never take meals one after another (indiscriminately) but whenever the stomach is cleansed (emptied)—unlike the merchant people who have a fixed time (for eating), nay, even a set hour which is never changed, as if the act of eating were some sacred duty to perform. The main thing to remember is that one's eating should be done after the stomach is

emptied but, naturally, all this depends on what was consumed, whether the day is long or short and on other external circumstances. The time to eat again is when the food already taken has left the stomach, when there is no aftertaste from belching (yawning) and when a real appetite is felt, i.e., when the mouth is filled with saliva—and even then one should wait another half an hour. Some say no less than two hours should go by from this point (before sitting down to the meal). This depends on the stoutness or leanness of the body, on the richness or thinness of its juices, on its warmth or cold, etc. The lean man whose body juices are sparse and warm should wait about half an hour before he resumes eating, the man of opposite qualities about two hours. This is the time limit for emptying the stomach, as explained above, and hunger alone is not to be relied upon, since people with stomach complaints (pancreatic disturbances) often experience false hunger caused by the bad, malignant juices which beset the sphincter duodeni (stomach outlet). It appears that those who are used to eating mornings and evenings, fare best when taking their meals, in wintertime, two or three hours after the coming of day, depending on the length of the night and their digestive powers. In summer one should take one's meal five hours after sunrise, because at that time the stomach empties (best). The evening meal, accordingly, should be taken long before the end of the day, as explained above. Note, that with those having (only) one meal a day it sometimes happens on (long) winter nights that they rise early in the night to empty their bowels. It also happens that these people take food out of their regular time, especially when days are long. Then, when bedtime arrives, their stomach is quite empty. These things are of frequent occurrence.

4. This I have proved to myself, both in theory and practice, by an experiment which I made on myself.* When I ate bread, even a little bit of it, it did me harm if taken out of time and my digestion weakened. When I fell asleep on an empty stomach bad juices were soon drawn into it, as happens with those who mortify their flesh (by fasting). So I found it expedient to control the rumblings of my stomach and pacify it, by the consumption of pleasing, easily digested food. Some times I took chicken soup and slept soundly afterwards. Another time I opened five or six eggs and ate their yolks together with some cane sugar or salt. Sometimes I ate some peanuts and raisins (without their pips) or sugar-coated almonds, or drank some sugared or honeyed drink (e.g., sakang'bin—honey-vinegar-lemon and water) which I happened to have with me. However, in the rainy season (winter) I have a few glasses of wine, depending on the degree of cold, just to avoid going to bed hungry, because in that case the stomach may be plagued with raw, unripe juices which need maturing.

5. All this I advise Your Highness to follow. Instead of wine on rainy days (which is unacceptable to Your Highness on religious grounds) drink one third up to half a liter (one tea glass) of a fine honey drink (non-alcoholic). This diet I find to be very useful.

---

* NOTE: Maimonides used to take only one meal a day, excepting the Sabbath. At night he had some tidbits, so as not to fall asleep on an empty stomach.

30

VII

Which Treats of Beverages

1. HAVING discussed the nature of the foods suitable for Your Highness I will say a few words about beverages, although most of them I do not apply to Moslems for whom wine[16] is forbidden. It concerns the kinds of wine (spirits) which come to the boil and mix rapidly and are of themselves forbidden to most people. From this the Almighty already safeguarded you enough, so that I have nothing to caution you against. It is true wine is injurious to all people, making them feel heavy, affecting their brain and hearing, even giving rise to severe diseases and aggravating the one under discussion; but it is the amount (of wine) which is to blame, apart from the drunkenness it brings about. However, a small quantity, some 3 or 4 glasses of wine taken at the time the food is digested and out of the stomach, (i.e., in the small intestine) is quite useful in the diet of the healthy and an excellent cure for many disorders. Its advantages lie in the fact that it affects the digestive process favorably, increases and raises native warmth, removes superfluous residue in the form of sweat and urine, etc. It is no use, though, to enumerate the good points of a thing whose enjoyment is out of the question where Your Highness is concerned. It is, however, of general knowledge that if taken in moderate measure and at the right time it is

beneficial in many respects to both body and soul, especially with regard to old people who would scarcely manage without it or similar measures. It should be emphasized, however, that too much of it corrupts the soul and body of people of all ages, from the day of their birth until the end of their lives.

2. Since it is forbidden to Moslems in either large or small amounts physicians have taken pains to put at their disposal similar beverages. Here belongs the honeyed drink (mead), seasoned with spices, so that it has most of the advantages of wine without "gladdening the heart," and it does away with superfluous residue and gases. I wish to recommend to Your Highness a certain recipe for such a drink, which I learned from my teachers, and which resembles (wine) to the highest degree.[17] I cite also a few spices which are useful for everybody and especially for Your Highness, since they stimulate urination.[18]

Take half a kab (1 liter) lentils (some say linseed), preferably the darker kind, rinse and immerse in 5 Egyptian liters of clear water for one night. On the following day cook until their strength passes to the liquid but do not wait until the lentils are completely done. Then the liquid is poured through a sieve unto one liter of the finest white bee honey, transferred (to a pot) and cooked over a small fire while skimming the froth all the time. After all the froth has been cleared add half an ounce borage (Borago officinalis), three parts[19] of mint, spices, and sweet scents, depending on the season[20] and one's physique. What I particularly recommend for Your Highness and the disease in question, and considering your body build and organs, is that to the lentils, at the time of immersion, half an ounce of pilsia (kuzbarath albir—Adianthum capillus veneris) should be added. After clearing the froth off the drink one should also add to it some anis (Anethum graveolens) mixed with 2 zuzim (ca. 8 grams) of arundo spice cane, crushed ginger, mastix (balsam of Pistacia lentiscus) muscat nuts, valeriana tuberosa (nard), about half a zuz each (ca. 2 grams), one fourth zuz of kurkuma (Crocus sativus). All this is forced again with a spoon through a cloth until it looks like a beverage, such as julep (from roses, sugar and water) and taken off the fire. No more than one liter of it should be concocted at one time, since when left over for long it flows over and undergoes fermentation. Its effect is admittedly somewhat weaker but it should be preferred to the fermented kind because it must not be diluted with water and so be of less use when drunk. Before going on a journey it should be mixed (on hot days) with cold water and in winter with hot water but not consumed soon after being mixed but an hour later, when it is well diluted. I think it advisable to add to it some mentastrum (Mentha aquatica) or some common mint (Mentha sativa), which assist digestion and clear the chest and lungs of residue.

3. Regarding water most people know that its consumption soon after meals neutralizes the food because it settles down between the stomach and the food with the food, as it were, floating upon it and staying mostly undigested. However, if Your Highness is used to it and feels well (drinking water soon after meals) then take of it as little as possible and as late as possible (after eating). The best time to drink water is about two hours after eating. It is well to drink sweet, clear and light water, free of any smell, fresh water drawn on the same day.[21] It is important that the water is boiled a little and drunk after it cools down, because in that condition it is much less harmful and offsets its

detrimental effect as explained above. If in the process of boiling a trace of liquiritia glabria is added to the water so little that it hardly affects its flavor and some muscat[22] to impart to the water its taste and aroma, and (the water) boiled again in a clean, covered vessel, the outcome is a drink fit for all healthy people in summer and winter. It strengthens the internal organs and invigorates the stomach.

Even a small amount of it is of much use.[23] People suffering from any complaint would do well to add to this water the cure which was prescribed for them. It should be noted that the drinking of tepid water, i.e., in which no trace of coolness is left, is extremely bad for the digestion of all people; it weakens the stomach and fails to quench a man's thirst even when taken profusely. On the other hand, cool water, i.e., such that people do not shrink from its cold, nor being icy cold, is the most recommended for drinking when thirsty, especially for people of warm temper.

4. Physicians are of the opinion that even of this fine water only a moderate amount should be taken, never too much. They say it assists digestion, helps the body to put on weight apart from food,[24] stimulates the appetite, makes for good looks, checks temperature and inflammatory diseases, keeps down heartburn (lahavat halev) and sepsis. Even a little bit of it is enough to quench a man's thirst. The effect of lukewarm water is just the opposite: it causes bodily weakness, loss of stamina and early anemia.[25] It is said of most peoples who use tepid water, i.e., such that is not cool, that they are deficient in blood, of lean physique, susceptible to diseases of the milt and the liver, have poor appetites and faces gloomy and lusterless, without any expression, because their blood is defective and exposed to inflam-

mations and infections of all kinds. Hence, it should be avoided at all cost.

5. Having laid down the dietary measures for eating and drinking we add to this discussion also regulations for physical exercise and rest. We pass on, as laid down before, to the remaining seven precepts* of good conduct.

---
* See chapter I.3.

VIII

*Which Treats of the Rules of Hygienic Conduct Regarding
Air and Psychic Moods*

1. IT IS WELL KNOWN that clean, fresh air free of any
contamination is advisable for all people, whether
healthy or sick. With the latter, however, the air should
be of such a temperature as to offset that of their disease, which is common to all things deviating from
their middle course. This means that on hot days the
air should be conditioned by spraying and sprinkling
the floor with scented water, by flowers, heat-abating
leaves, and draft. Conversely, on cold, rainy days the
air should be fumigated with perfumes tending to warm
up the organism or by the application of herbs which
absorb humidity and act as drying agents. Cold, humid
air is very harmful for Your Highness. Also, avoid as
much as possible both cold and warm urine stimu-
lants.[26]

2. As for the effect of psychic moods it is generally
acknowledged that the impact of mental suffering,
agitation, and obstinacy is to impair mental activity and
physical well-being so much so that one's appetite for
food is completely lost when in mental anguish, fear,
mourning, or distress. In such a condition a man cannot
even use his voice properly because his agitation affects
his respiratory organs and he cannot exercise them at
will. The weight of the accumulated gas residue within

him keeps him from walking erect, standing in an upright position and inhaling a sufficient volume of air. He experiences difficulty in exercising his other organs as well. Should this condition endure a man cannot avoid falling ill and if it takes on a chronic character death is not long in coming. All this is universally known and should not detain us here. On the other hand, gaiety and liveliness have the opposite effect; they gladden the heart, stimulate the movement (circulation) of the blood and the degree of mental activity stemming from such a condition is in some cases among the highest.

However, when people indulge to excess, in headlong pursuit of pleasure, which sometime happens with the ignorant and the foolish, they too invariably fall sick and may even sink altogether because in that case their soul is burdened with decay and hastens to leave the body, their hearts fail to function and death becomes inevitable.

3. The cure of these two kinds of psychic states and their prevention, so that a man shall not fall a prey to them, lies not in food recipes, neither in drugs alone, nor in regular medical advice. The cure of such conditions belongs rather to other spheres of professional knowledge, by which we mean the philosophical virtues taught by the philosophers who are engaged in the study of ethics, morals, etc. Undoubtedly, these psychological methods are a greater help in these emotional disorders and a better safeguard against them for they uncover the nature of such conditions and the best way to cure them by learning from experience and failure. Furthermore, the philosophical virtues guard a man against extreme emotional states. They keep a man from falling into brutish emotionalism on mournful or joyous occa-

sions as happens with the ignorant multitude. A man so treated reveals his mental state by resorting to friendly counsel, not by a show of explosive action, enervating anguish and the like.* The same effects are possessed by moral and ethical teachings. A man should take easily the world and its phenomena and what passes for luck and ill luck. In reality these are as nothing. They are hardly to be noticed. There is no comfort in the one nor alarm in the other. In the world of our mind they are no more than ludicrous, idle specters which vanish away.

4. All this I have mentioned knowing well that normally it does not occur in such treatises. I have done this on purpose because I wish Your Highness real and lasting happiness and would spare you serious trouble. I know Your Highness is gravely afflicted and, what is more, that mere diet and medical treatment cannot fully cure this disorder. For a man like Your Highness it is fitting that he adopt these prophylactic measures and follow in the footsteps of the just and (learned) prophets, laugh at death in his face and follow the laws of nature and necessity. Let Your Highness occupy himself with things useful and keep away from things useless and may God show you the path of truth.

---

* Regarding the effect on the nervous system and gland secretion cf. Maimonides' Regimen sanitatis IV 1. and my note there. S.M.

IX

Which Treats of Hygiene for Retention and Discharge of Juices

1. USEFUL DIETARY RULES for everybody, especially for one in whose body bad juices have accumulated, imply also that the stool be always soft or nearly so. Forced evacuation, even of a few days' duration, has a general weakening effect.[27] This is why Ibn Zohar advises maintaining a soft discharge, recommending as follows: crush 10 zuzim (ca. 40 grams) of Indian date (tamarind), submerge in warm water, add 3/4 zuz (3 grams) ground rhubarb;[28] after 24 hours dissolve in an ounce of lemon-peel juice and you have a clear palatable drink.

2. Says the Author: The above I prescribe for people with thin juices or for the young and in warm climates. However, for those plagued with thick, slimy juices, for old people, and particularly for those suffering from the disease this book has been written for, I suggest the remedy recommended by Galen. This remedy is prepared from the inner parts of dried figs, wild-growing olives,[29] raisins, and the small fruit of dogwood.[30] The manner of preparation is this: take core of safflower seed (Carthamus tinctorius, 5 zuzim (20 grams, 1/8 zuz 1/2 gram) edible salt, core of dried figs 20 zuzim (80 grams); grind in a stone or wooden mortar until a compact mass is obtained. All this taken with a mouthful of

39

warm water has a strong softening effect on the stool. According to Galen, it is among the best remedies for old people. Another remedy is to crush the small dogwood cherries[31] and press through a sieve together with 2 ounces of bee honey, which make the stool tolerably easy. Another effective measure is swallowing a nutful of radish juice.[32] This cures without causing any damage, cleanses all the inner organs and thins the secretions of liver, spleen, kidneys, bladder, and lungs. This remedy should be taken regularly.[33]

3. Says the Author: The same effect is ascribed to beet juice which should be added as spice to porridge with much olive oil. The liquid, too, is of curative value.[34] Similarly effective is a concoction popular in Egypt. It is prepared from lemonade, the core of safflower seed and beet and is a sure combination to soften the stool of most people. Another purgative is honey water boiled with berries of the cordia myxa[34a] and the acacia (Acacia aegyptica, el quarad.[35] This, strained on sugar and oil of sweet almonds, softens the stool and lets the waste matter slip through easily. Of all these formulas one should pick out the one suitable for one's organism, according to one's age and season of the year.

4. A man suffering from a diarrhea of two to three days' duration should have his food limited and given instead some common astringents such as those prepared from the sumac fruit (Rhus coriaria), half-matured dates, and raisins, pomegranates and beet ribs, cooked in quince and juice of roses.

5. Generally speaking, one should try regulating one's stool by sticking to the same food. One should take as little as possible of apple cider in quince juice or similar potions which make for constipation, even if one is used

to them. Of these a man should take only what suits him best, depending on his age and the season of the year. As for quantity there is no need to consult a doctor, because it varies as the case may be.

This is common knowledge with most educated people in all countries who have had anything to do with medicine. However, the important thing to watch and consider at all times and rely on expert medical advice is the purging with violent medicines entailing spasms, such as coloquintida, fruit of convolvulus, turpethus (turbid vegetabile) and the resin,*36 (from the root of Convulvulus scammonia) and the like, especially with old men. Regarding these people Galen cautions in the strongest words against purgatives of this kind; neither is it advisable to use strong measures to stop diarrhea; they should consult a skilled physician who can consider all the circumstances of the case.

6. Discharge by enema, on the other hand, is among the best methods in prevention and cure alike and exceptionally effective in emptying the juices. Even when the enema is administered together with spasmogenic drugs it does no harm to the vital organs and gives rise to no pain as is the case with purgatives. Relief is assured and the discharge is easy. If one intends but to loosen and remove hardened waste matter the enema is among the most ancient[37] and time-proven hygienic measures. When this is used no medicines are necessary, since they weaken the inner lining of the intestines and cause vomiting like most laxatives taken by mouth.

In his book (*De Clystiribus*)[38] Galen has recommended some remedies for hardened, solid stool difficult to discharge. These are: Two ounces of honey, half a liter (ca. 192 grams) water, one ounce fine olive oil, 1

* cf. my commentary to Regimen sanitatis, p. 126. S.M.

zuz (4 grams) natron—all warmed and used as an enema. The harder the stool the more oil should be added. If the removal of raw masses of phlegm is aimed at, more honey and natron should be given.

7. Another remedy is half a liter of beet juice and 2 ounces of fine olive oil. Warm and apply in enema. Still another is wheat bran covered with water, boiled until one third of the liquid evaporates, then strained until a sticky mass is obtained. Add oil and use for enema. This is effective in emptying dried matter. All these formulas are from Galen and I endorse them heartily. Likewise effective is an enema with sap of linseed and fenugreek (Trigonella foenumgraecum) or both, with oil and chicken fat with an admixture of beet juice.[39] These are good combinations which always clear the feces without being irritating or painful. If, in addition to that, some honey or honey cake is given to old people (by mouth), the effect is most beneficial. This too is recommended by Galen.

8. Galen mentions the fact that an enema with liquid linseed is useful for tubercular (phtisic) patients, since it mitigates the bad juices. Note that the regular use of enema purifies the brain, liquifies intestinal matter, prevents premature aging, assists digestion and wards off many diseases and this is because it cleans and flushes from below and the upper organs get a clear way before them to dispose of the waste matter along the channels provided by very nature. And so everything fits in as explained above.

9. NOTE: In encouraging disease there is no better method than the obstruction of the natural outlet of the two (prime) excretions of the body (stool and urine). Galen has explained that the feces are forced back by

the wind, (pneuma), lose liquid content with the gases mounting to the brain, rottenness steps in marked by a loss of digestion and an onset of severe diseases. The same happens when urine is kept back. We give but a few intimations of this danger but it should be taken care of strictly.

10. Vomiting belongs to the rules of general hygiene everybody should live by and pay attention to, especially in this disease. In keeping healthy one should always resort to (artificial) vomiting unless one is unaccustomed to it or suffering from some cerebral or eye disease. The reason for vomiting, in my opinion, is because superfluous residue cannot help forming in the stomach and the intestines. Phlegm is a form of raw mucus. When this residue is left behind in the stomach and the intestines after the first digestion it places itself between the food and the lining of those organs. Thereby digestion is hampered, part of the food remains undigested. As for the intestines divine providence equipped then with the outlet of the bile channel which provides them with green bile. This washes away the phlegm, liquifying it and cleansing the intestines. The stomach, however, is never entered by the bile, because, if it were, great damage would be done, as explained by Galen. This is why we must rely on man's artifice and clear the stomach by vomiting.

11. Galen says as follows: The cleaning of the stomach is complete only with some people.[40] The ancient Egyptians,[41] therefore, were certainly right when they included in their rule of hygiene the prescription to cause vomiting after a meal at least once a month. Some find it salutary to clean their stomach even twice a month. All agree that before vomiting some sharp flavored food should be taken because of its purging

effect. This is done in order to clear the stomach contents from phlegm before damage is done to the whole organism, through nausea generated by the sharp foods, since they all form green bile and are injurious to health.

12. Says the Author: The fact is that a great many people are fond of spicy, pungent food such as heavily salted cheese, fish or meat jelly[45] food giving off a smell, such as kamka (mouldy bread or fruit steeped in vinegar), all kinds of leeks, of sour milk, radish, onion, and similar foods. The reason therefor is this: In a man's stomach phlegm is gradually building up and one longs for things which might render it harmless and dissolve it. Thus, when the stomach is cleaned by vomiting, as Galen suggests, or by purgatives or other remedies[43] fed into it, the phlegm dissolves and the juices no longer intervene between the food and the stomach lining and there is no craving for those bad foods—that is, unless such a liking already exists.

13. I do not know Your Highness' habit regarding vomiting. If it comes easily to you[44] then do it in the customary way used for clearing the stomach and ridding it of superfluous residue, namely: take two or three peeled radishes,[45] crush with some nuts, boil one ounce of dill in one liter of water, pour contents on the crushed radish together with two[46] ounces of bee's honey and one ounce of sharp vinegar or more, depending on its acidity, then let stand overnight. On the following morning the emetic is taken before regular mealtime. Then some unleavened bread is taken with various dishes, such as salt herring, fish-jelly, watermelon, berkok plums (praecoccia, Prunus armeniaca) when in season, radish, onion, leek (Allium porrum), honey,

bean dish sholet,* or oatmeal with husks. All these and similar dishes are conducive to vomiting. They fill the stomach and should be kept there for a while.[47] Vomiting is best done in a raised position, so that nothing stays back in the stomach, usually about noon. In winter time, vomiting is best done in the bath; one should rest afterwards and consume nothing until really hungry. When thirsty some apple cider may be taken; when real hunger sets in a young hen or turtle dove and meat broth.[48] In a few days the after-effects of vomiting are past, as soon as the stomach recovers from it. Some people find it easy to vomit on oxymel (sakang' bin), honey, vinegar concoction and warm tea. Others vomit from the smell of oats alone or after drinking beer or wine in sufficient quantities. All this is true. For those who vomit with difficulty or are unaccustomed to it or avoiding it on doctor's orders because of some faulty organ or bad constitution, I prescribe every five days one ounce of rose juice boiled with sugar and one ounce of the sharp oxymel (sakang'bin) mixed in psyllinum seed (Plantago psyllium). After a while food is taken, preferably coarse, and tasting sour. This clears the stomach of phlegm without having to vomit.

14. When the organism is humid (juicy), such as in youngsters and with those of phlegmatic body build, one should swallow slowly one ounce of oxymel dressed with onion[49] together with one ounce of rose syrup cooked with honey. A man of cold temper having in his stomach a big accumulation of phlegm (white bile) should add to the above some ginger syrup cooked with honey or half a zuz (2 grams) plain ginger. Those of warm temper and still young should take one ounce

* Grissin shel pul—often recurring in the Mishna, Nidda 9, Machshirim 5, a.o.

cooked rose syrup and one ounce lemonade every five days. All this clears the stomach of phlegm (white bile) and one is not dependent on vomiting in cases where it has been contraindicated, as explained above.

15. The following experiment I made on myself: I took one ounce of white sugar, on cold seasons crushed with half a zuz (2 grams) of anis, on hot days absorbed with some lemonade, every third or fourth day, as the case may be. I found out it cleans the stomach of phlegm and the diaphragm as well. The same effect was produced by sharp (wine), oxymel dressed with quince or quince lemonade. In a few days my digestion was much improved and the stomach cleared of accumulated phlegm. This is prepared as follows: Some fine quince, not too astringent and rather hard, not too sour, and half boiled with froth skimmed away. Of this a liter (ca. 325 grams) is taken, vinegar added half a liter (165 grams), sugar and skimmed honey mixture four liters (1300 grams); all this is poured into a second vessel and held on fire and supplemented with one zuz (4 grams) white pepper and 2 zuzim (8 grams) ginger. Should this not be enough to produce nausea, more is added depending on the degree of cold of both temper and climate. Sometimes mere lemonade is sufficient. Although this cannot compete in effectiveness with vinegar in dilution of juices and the cure of constipation and rot it is still milder on the joints and nerves.

16. The use of urine-stimulation, bloodletting and purgatives in general hygiene is based on a great error[50] and has never been suggested by a physician worthy of the name. Bloodletting and purgatives should be resorted to only in case of illness, when necessitated by some glut, i.e., it is used only when the body is bloated with bad juices or when blood pressure rises, the blood

is agitated and seething because of bad composition or faulty functioning. Those who resort to bloodletting or "cleansing remedies" (hygiene) at set intervals might better retain the habit but by all means increase the intervals from time to time and gradually reduce the discharge until they reach old age, when this practice comes to an end.*

---

* The text could equally well be rendered: "This practice of bloodletting and purgatives is already outmoded."

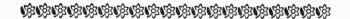

X

Which Treats of the Hygiene of Sleeping, of Waking, of the Bath, of Massage and of Coitus

1. SLEEP in this disease is rather harmful, especially during an attack and particularly so soon after a meal. Those afflicted (with this disease) should therefore sleep as little as possible. Note: Going to sleep immediately after having eaten is harmful to anybody, especially to Your Highness, because (in such a state) the brain fills with vapors. However, should it be a habit with you (taking a nap after meals) I suggest Your Highness occupy himself with something for a while in an upright position so as to avoid the injurious effect of breaking a habit abruptly, i.e., you should gradually extend the interval between eating and falling asleep up to three to four hours. After that time sleep contributes to the completion of the digestive process and assists in the digestion of the rest of the food residue which remains in the stomach. The main thing is to proceed carefully with habits affecting health; even if they have a bad effect they should not be discarded suddenly[50a] (for the sake of good habits but the latter should be allowed time to fit in with a man's disposition smoothly and naturally).

2. Your Highness would certainly come across this feeling in the course of time when you take up the proposed

health regimen. However, while the cure is progressing Your Highness should in no way consider any change of habit but adhere to it with the greatest care. Of the good points of habit Galen speaks in his book *De usu partium*, saying this: Each man has his peculiar habits the breaking of which is fraught with the greatest danger, which holds good not only with regard to convalescents and the like but to sick men under treatment as well.

3. Washing (with cold water) is not advisable for Your Highness because cold water is very injurious in this disorder, contracting the pores and retarding the dissolution or disruption of the phlegm which plays an important part in this disease. Profuse bathing, too, is dangerous in this condition. From this[51] however, people abstain of their own accord, especially before and during the onset of an attack. Your Highness should beware of it, even if much given to it. In the latter case the interval between bathing should be prolonged to a day and the duration of the bath gradually reduced. Your Highness should take great pains to exclude the risk of a cold draught while issuing from the bath and never bathe on an empty stomach.[52] Before[53] leaving the bathroom Your Highness should indulge in a short nap, say one hour, which always benefits any man who wants his thick, slimy juices to bring to the boil especially in this disease.

4. Says Galen: It is worthwhile to know that no medicine can top an afterbath nap in respect of digestive processes, particularly with regard to the dissolution of bad juices.

5. Says the Author: Being aware of this I used to take a bath at sunset only upon which I went directly to

bed and was soon fast asleep. I learned to appreciate the wisdom of this counsel. It is important not to step into a bathing basin or tub filled with cold water; the latter must be warm enough to make one recoil at first. It is very good if the water contains some salt, too. Salt[54] makes for rapid drying up of the body and reduces its humidity. Note: Profuse bathing is injurious to all men because it undermines the bodily juices and precipitates their decay.

Physicians of our time, however, are of the opinion that the restriction of bathing to one bath in every ten days is rather exaggerated[55] but in this regard opinions vary with the varying countries, dispositions and customs. Much of this we have discussed already in our book *Regimen sanitatis*.*[56] Here only this may be said: The flushing of the body with lukewarm water is outright dangerous because it increases the humidity of the brain and impedes its functioning. Likewise, the abrupt use of cold water on the head is highly injurious to the organism, because it cools the brain (rapidly) and blocks the discharge of residue from the head. On the other hand, washing with hot water is highly recommended. The heat should be so great as to rubify the skin of the head. This contributes to the warming up the brain, smoothing its operation and reducing the residue trapped in it. The turgor of a man's skin becomes tougher and more resistant so that one does not fall sick on the slightest occasion. These rules Your Highness should observe with the greatest care.

6. Rubbing up of the entire body at the beginning of the day, on waking up, and the massaging of the arms and legs before going to bed is good hygiene for any

* Maimonides' most interesting treatise on the hygiene of both body and soul, published by Mossad Harav Kook, Jerusalem, 1957

man on healthy days. Doctors' opinions vary with regard to massaging and the time it should be undertaken. A description of these practices lies outside the scope of the present book, just as we refrained from bringing up everything worth saying with regard to bodily exercise[57] and massage in our book *Regimen sanitatis*. Suffice it that I have hinted in this book at what should be done in this respect.

Regarding the disease Your Highness is beset with, modern doctors also advocate the massaging of the chest. In this respect there is no divergence of opinion. Therefore I shall limit myself to a description of the chief methods of massaging procedure mentioned by Galen. Next I shall advise Your Highness when chest massaging might be of benefit to you and when it should be avoided.

7. Regarding this Galen says the following: With debilitated persons massaging of the body should not be undertaken during an attack, when the disease is rampant and explosive. On healthy days, however, such patients would do well to indulge in it more than usual, especially dry massaging. Sometimes pain is felt in some organ from this type of massage[58] but this serves to prevent its recurrence later on, especially when the massage is applied 2 to 3 hours before the anticipated attack. This is explained by the fact that the vigor of such affected organ is heightened and the supply of pathogenous juices to it is blocked by the above procedure. This is equally true with regard to people of advanced or any other age. When it comes to exercising diseased organs my advice is to tamper less with old people than with others. The best thing to do with regard to the former is to leave their affected organs as much at rest as possible.

8. Says the Author: It appears from the above that the massaging of the chest between attacks or shortly before a new attack is absolutely harmless,[59] provided the massage is applied not later than 2 hours before the onset. Another point of importance: Never overstrain the diseased organs of old people.

9. Regarding coitus it is well known, even to the general public, that it is harmful to most people and, when indulged in to excess, is injurious to all of them. Discharge of semen as such is not counted among the salutary precepts of hygiene, except with a limited number of people with a wrong juice combination who change as time goes on. Along with the semen vital juices[60] cannot help escaping from the body, so that its chief organs dry up and cool gradually. Only young men bear well this unavoidable nuisance, although even among them many pay for it with sickness. In any case, to old people coitus is at all times harmful since they are dependant on anything that increases their natural warmth and keeps their organs properly humid while coitus tends to extinguish and sap their strength little by little, as we pointed out above. A man of advanced age should therefore abstain from its exercise, the more strictly the better. All this is part of a healthy hygiene. Besides, this is also tied up with questions of keeping the body free of infections, purification of the spirit and of acquiring virtues through continence, modesty, and piety. If we say of coitus that it has an injurious effect on all organs it is especially true with regard to the brain because the main discharge has to do with this part of the body. All this has been discussed by Hippocrates. This is why it is so important for any one suffering from repeated headache to keep away from coitus. A man given to excessive exercise of coitus is found on inspection to suffer from (premature) lapses

of memory and mental debility,[61] with faulty digestion combined with green sickness, defective vision and bad appearance. There is a good reason for it, and, since human behavior varies greatly as well as human temperaments, there are admittedly some people, indifferent or subject to bad humor or defective digestion who actually happen to regain by it their vitality, cheerfulness, and good appetite, while others experience just the opposite. People's peculiarities vary much in this respect. Galen described one of the bad aspects of this problem, saying: There is a physical phenomenon which should be regarded as very unfortunate, namely, that some people seem to produce a lot of warm semen which keeps them permanently excited and eager to discharge it. When they do discharge it their stomach as well as their entire organism weaken, they dry up and grow lean, their looks deteriorate and their eyes sink deep in their sockets. Such people, even when they limit or suspend their coitus of their own accord because of the discomfort that comes over them, often suffer from a sense of heaviness in their head and pain in their stomach, which means that even continence brings them no relief. This results from the fact that they are harassed with nightly pollutions. Thus pollution causes them no less harm than coitus itself.

10. Says the Author: My reason for mentioning the above was to draw attention to the various reactions of people in this respect. This book does not intend to offer medical details of all the cases involved and their treatment.

In short, Your Highness may carry on in this regard more or less as you are used to but would do well to diminish your coitus little by little, as I said before, which is fitting in this disease and, depending on one's age, salutary for all people. Note: Coitus is bad for all

53

people if it takes place soon after a bath or following physical exercise, at daybreak[62] or within two days of the drinking of asparagus[63] (a diaphoretic), to prevent two kinds of discharge (sweat, semen) from coinciding and enervating the organism all at once. Further, it is not advisable to have coitus when hungry, neither when the stomach is replete with food, but at the time the food has left the upper stomach and before hunger has set in again. The evil attending coitus on an empty stomach is much greater than occurring in a state of repletion. The exercise of coitus while seriously ill is outright dangerous, even deadly. This I happened to observe myself and also learned from reliable information that a man once had coitus while in acute fever and his strength ebbed on that very day. He finally suffered a heart attack and died on the following night.[64]

11. Having concluded these chapters which form, as it were, a set of rules of hygiene and dietary prescriptions we proceed now to a description of the remedies called for in this disease and of what should be done at the time of attack, before, or shortly after it.

XI

Which Treats of Remedies Against This Disease

1. USEFUL AS A preventive measure in this condition is the care for the restoration of proper brain functioning[65] by the use of combined remedies which contribute to the draining of the turbid juices. Next comes the care for the cleansing of the lungs. In the strengthening of the brain to prevent it from harboring, producing, and discharging any residue, and the strength of each particular organ to forestall any damage to some vital part,* care should be taken to have any lurking residue completely ejected and the normal balance (mixture) restored. Every organ as a rule does away with bad residue when it regains its normal mixture thereby enhancing its functioning power.[66] When it is in a sick condition, however, and we are ourselves trying to fortify it until its natural mixture is restored, we must include in our drugs something of curative value, as is appropriate. A description of these drugs would require too much time and space and is outside the scope of the present book.

2. Physicians before us have prescribed restorative remedies for a number of symptoms characterizing this

---

* In medieval times distinction was made between *eivarim* or *kelim kilyiim* (vital organs such as brain, heart, and liver) and *kelim mitdamiyim* (less important organs such as arms, legs, and nose).

disease; all of them are agreed on the desirability of resorting to rubricating measures for the head, even if they are highly caustic. Their purpose is to prevent catarrh (flow). This treatment would be hardly applicable in your case because your brain is warm as it is and any further heating will bring about additional deterioration of its strength—even if it dries up the diseased matter, dispels it and keeps it from flowing out. In earlier times doctors also ordered certain powders and salves for fortifying the brain in this disease; these however have a warming effect and anything resembling them are inadvisable for Your Highness. On the other hand, considering the nature of this disorder, cooling remedies to fortify the brain are also inadmissible. Because of the inadvisability of these extremes therapy is rather difficult in your case and mistakes are easily made. Your Highness would therefore do well to use various remedies of a changing character. In any case, lung clearing requires sharp, expectorative measures. But Galen and all his successors have always taken care that such remedies generate no excessive heat and have a particularly diluting action so that the lung juices do not combine with them,[67] the sputum is dissolved, and thus the matter does not become hardened, sticky and difficult to discharge. In any case, moisture content in such remedies should be pronounced to ease expectoration. The same applies to catarrh. Sometimes the discharge from the brain is pathogenic and the cause of illness and sleeplessness, and sometimes it causes pressure and tension when it reaches the lungs. Sometimes the flow is sharp and rough,[68] necessitating, in spite of the existent catarrh, some breaking up with a diluting agent, i.e., making for a worse catarrh. On other occasions, that which comes down from the head is cold and thick, even if the brain stays warm. Things like this are common with all

56

organs, often because the residue kept in a subsidiary organ is contrary to that of a main part. Again, occasionally the matter reaching the lungs is thin and liquid and cannot be expelled until it thickens and acquires a glutinous quality. As far as I know your case is different. Since the situation is so changeable it is important that Your Highness agree to be under constant observation by a specialist who can always come up with the proper remedy. Such a physician would stick to some set treatment until he decides to change it for another, to adopt one course or two such therapies simultaneously, prescribing a single drug which combines both procedures, and basing himself, as Your Highness saw for himself, on authoritative sources. Anything[69] Your Highness reports on the symptoms of the disease must be duly considered by such physicians.

3. The mere empiricists who do not think scientifically are greatly in error. Sometimes they succeed by pure chance, sometimes they fail, again by chance. This is why I always maintain: He who puts his life in the hands of a physician skilled in his art but lacking scientific training is not unlike the mariner who puts his trust in good luck, relying on the sea winds which know no science to steer by. Sometimes they blow in the direction the seafarer wants them to blow, and then his luck shines upon him; another time they may spell his doom. Let Your Highness beware of it. Many people have paid with their lives at the hands of such practitioners and practices. Those who could save themselves did so, those who could not succumbed, all entirely by chance.

4. This is also implied by Hippocrates when he says: Experience (alone) is fraught with danger. This is also how Galen and many of his disciples understand it.

Medicines should be compounded scientifically and logically, in accord with the particular qualities of this or that person. In this disease the following remedies might be mentioned: Enemas which are of use at the time of onset in draining the thick juices, smelling herbs to fortify the brain and dry out any humidity lurking in it and to prevent any flow coming out of it. I shall mention two, three or more remedies advisable in each particular treatment, all suitable in your case and answering your juice combination and Your Highness may rely on them wholeheartedly. Sometimes one of them should be applied, sometimes the other. An opinion endorsed by the best physicians anywhere, particularly in this disease, is to proceed from one medicine to another, although the curative power of the various combined remedies is almost the same in each of them. It is not my intention, however, to enlarge upon a description of the same. The sequence of medicines to be followed by Your Highness is first to fortify the brain with the prescription I gave you in the chapter on combined remedies, then to purge it with medicines also described therein. There are numerous formulas for that. This Your Highness should do twice a year when you have a feeling of being bloated with bad juices. Should you feel better, once a year is quite all right, about April. The same holds good with regard to the liquid medicine, which should be taken when feeling crammed with food. I am sure that if Your Highness would follow the rules I recommended one treatment a year would be quite enough, around April, using a mild purgative. In case of an attack Your Highness should drink first some of the beverages which I am going to describe, starting with the less refined.[70] The foods, on the other hand, are much lighter. Of the beverages I prefer only those with sugar, some chicken soup, then infusions which I mentioned while speaking of the remedies to ease expectoration. In the evening preceding the attack, before going to bed, some sweetened barley porridge should be taken if in fever, and some broth of old chicken if not. Should this be enough to clear the lung and allay the attack no other remedies are required. However, should it prove to be insufficient, the lungs remaining blocked and the attack continuing, then proceed to the next medicine, of stronger effect. Should all these liquid remedies fail an enema should be applied, of those mentioned before, again starting with the mildest. If weakened[71] by such procedure no laxative drink should be taken. Should all this not suffice (with no weakness felt) Your Highness should proceed to a laxative such as those I describe later on, which have only a local effect.[72]

5. Again, start with the mildest of emetics, some barley soup. If relief is felt, nothing else should be done, if not proceed to the next stronger emetic. In addition to that care should be taken to strengthen the brain with smelling herbs, and spices for fumigation, besides spoonfuls of medicines to clear the lungs. When the lung is eased the catarrh will stop of itself. So long as the catarrh is present and Your Highness feels the flow coming down do not turn to any other treatment until it is mitigated by the use of a medicine I shall describe below, otherwise the lungs become blocked for good and the patient gasps for breath. In such an emergency the lungs should be cleansed little by little by means of the remedies I cited above. Should this condition deteriorate, which God forbid, then turn to emetics, one after the other (until relief is obtained). In all these conditions it is important to abstain from prolonged sleep, especially from sleep during the day. In any case, sleep should not be courted but actually delayed

59

as much as possible, then taken in a sitting position. One should sleep tucked in all around (so as not to fall off the bed). Your Highness should beware of the use of bad (unboiled) water and even so should drink only when considerable thirst is felt. Likewise, beware of excessive bathing and physical exercise. Light exercise making little demand on the organism is of benefit during an attack.[73]

XII

Which Treats of Combined Remedies

THESE REMEDIES are of use in this affliction[74] and are referred to[75] but not necessarily described in the present book. These include drugs which require cooking, to ease expectoration and to clean the lungs, as well as those classed as purgatives.

1. The first remedy to resort to at the onset of an attack, is as follows: Liquiritia, althaea (Borago officinalis), 2 zuzim (8 grams) of each, fleabane (puleg'ia)[76] 3 zuzim, newly gathered fennel 6 inner parts all boiled and strained into freshly made julep (rosewater syrup). Another similar remedy is a handful of green fennel, ten dried figs, 4 zuzim of fleabane[77] all boiled together, strained, and consumed with sugar, honey and the like.

1a. Another, stronger remedy is fleabane (Mentha pulegia) 4 zuzim, skin of fennelroots, 3 zuzim; liquiritia and althaea, 2 zuzim of each; althaea root, lemon peel, 1 shekel (ca 16 grams) each; seeded raisins 1-2 ounce, all boiled together, strained and drunk with sugared water or julep (rosewater). To increase its expectorative power, strain in sakang'bin liquor (oxymel—honey vinegar).

1b. Another, still stronger remedy which clears the lungs of any deposit of raw phlegm: Ocimum basilicum[78] and Mentha pulegium[79] 3 zuzim of each; dried

61

hyssop 2 zuzim; Lavendula stoechas, Damascene ginger, (otherwise called Rassin and known to the Egyptian doctors[80] under the name of G'anach), Satureia hortensis,[81] 1 shekel of each; 6 figs all brought to the boil and strained on bee honey. This is not to be taken when in fever.

1c. Another remedy more potent than the above: Thymus capitatus, liquiritia (Prassion), Marubium vulgare,[82] Rubia tinctorum—of each one zuz; resin and fine bark of balsam tree, Valeriana tuberosa, 4 zuzim of each; mentastrum (Mentha silvestris) camomile root (Satureia hortensis[83],—2 zuzim of each; dried figs and seeded raisins,—5 zuzim of each, all brought to the boil and strained on oxymel. This has a strong purging effect and prevents head catarrh. It is not to be taken when in fever. In the case of fever and thin, sickly flow only the usual liquid remedies should be resorted to namely: Mentha pulegium,[84] liquiritia, bouglosses, endive seed, fennel, freshly gathered or dried waterbells, seed of Cucumis sativus, Eruca sativa,[85] Cordia myxa (sabistan), Sempervivum arboreum,[86] whichever happens to be in season. No exact quantity required and all are made up into a kind of pap and drunk with oxymel or violet syrup.[87] Also, other concoctions based on violet syrup (from either fresh or dried violets) may be given, depending on the state of temperature as judged by the physician. In case of slight fever seeded raisins or figs may safely be added. Says Razis: Any patient suffering from this disease, when given spleenwort, known as aqraban, in a potion based on figs, gets rid of his decayed phlegm at once; a wonderful remedy!

2. Says the Author: Razis' practical suggestion is also supported by theoretical (scientific) reasoning. What

we in the West use and apply, as the case may be, to clear the lungs of moisture, ease respiration and banish the cough is as follows: soak wheat bran for a night in hot water, force the pap through a sieve and add sugar and almond oil; then put it on the fire until it looks like a julep. Drink when it is lukewarm. Its beneficial effect is heightened when finely ground bitter or sweet almonds are included as well. Liquiritia,[88] too may be soaked together with the wheat bran. All these combinations are highly effective in this disease, widely used and require no precautionary measures, even when in fever.

3. Now we come to the infusions which clear the lungs by stirring up their diseased contents, ease expectoration and have a salutary effect on heavy breathing; they may be taken throughout the illness, any time during the day or night, and are as follows:

3a. Equal parts of seeded raisins and fenugreek cooked in clear water, sifted, strained, and left to stand for a long time. This may be taken several times a day, warmed up. Galen speaks very highly of this remedy. Later physicians however recommend another combination, namely: Fenugreek and figs cooked together, strained and made up with honey into a kind of spoon-fed medicine. Galen suggests a stronger formula: Crush bulbus scillae and add to the juice an equal part of honey, which yields a liquid medicine to be taken before and after meals one ounce at a time. Another potent remedy, also by Galen, is the following: Equal parts of Mentha aquatica and Mentha silvestris, Thymus capitatus, sassan roots (Iris), white pepper ripe seeds of Piper nigrum, roasted anise—all crushed and coarsely sifted, kneaded in cooked honey and an amount the size of a nut consumed each time.

3b. Later physicians recommend a still stronger formula: Round aristolochia, fenugreek, well ground, 3 ounces of each; myrrh, 2 ounces; rubia tinctorum, safran, 1 ounce; all crushed and taken in doses the size of a nut. A lighter and better remedy, likewise recommended by them and especially suitable in your case, is as follows: Take some big pine fruit rich in resin, cook in freshly gathered Marrubium vulgare, about half the quantity of the fruit, strain, add some pure honey and again put on fire until it acquires a honey-like consistency. Its salutary effect on the chest is wonderful to behold. A decoction used by Your Highness whenever warranted by the state of your health is made up of 1 ounce of sifted liquiritia juice and 2 ounces each of bitter, shelled almonds and sugar-icing (fanid). The almonds are crushed altogether and the whole mass dissolved in fennel water and cooked on a slow fire. For my part, I prefer an infusion of lemonade based on sand-like effervescent powder and cooked with Ocimum basilicum and almond oil.[89] This yields a highly effective remedy against any condition.

4. I regard it as my duty to remind Your Highness as well as to caution you in respect of the regular use of poppy drinks,[90] described by Galen. The good points of such beverages lie in preventing catarrh, making for restful sleep, banishing thinly flowing matter and easing expectoration. Here is the formula: Liquiritia, 10 zuzim; poppy, perfectly ripe white nuts;[91] 10 heads of Trochisci vegetabiles all crushed to a seed-like form and soaked in warm water for the night; the next morning it is cooked and filtered with 1 liter (325 grams) of grape juice or 1 liter of sugar and 1 liter of bee honey. When necessary, take by spoonful. A beverage containing honey is quite good for the lungs but inadvisable in cases of warm, raw-flowing[92]

catarrh; the one based on grapejuice forestalls catarrh while the one with sugar has a middling effect. When the catarrh takes on a milder form or stops altogether, or eventually moves to another organ[93] leaving the lungs relatively free of phlegm Your Highness should stop using these concoctions. In such a case the matter in the lung has become diluted so much that it is unable to escape and needs some thickening agent. The procedure is as following: Take tragacanth, gummi arabicum, crush and stir in above concotion on slow fire, and take when hot. Next take equal parts of poppy seed, alcohol, sugar, chalwa (from almonds) and starch;[94] crush everything in the juice of plantago psyllium seed, try it before use or knead the (poppy) seed in the thick juice of cucumber seed. To all this violet syrup may be added.

5. I myself once made up a remedy for a woman after having examined her condition thoroughly. My purpose was to purge her lungs, fortify her brain and stop her catarrh. Her constitution was moderately warm. At the time I discovered her disease she happened to have her period,[94a] her brain was not warm, neither too cool. Her body had little fat on it. At the time of onset she found the medicine a great help, and when she took to using it also on normal days the attacks were spaced at longer intervals and finally her improvement was such that she had one attack a year, later on only one in two years. And even then the attack was of a mild form. In making out my prescription I never lost sight of Galen's saying that the secret of therapeutic success lies in the heterogeneous effect of the combined ingredients which are dissimilar to each other in nature as well as in degree. Here is the recipe: I took some Ocimum basilicum and steeped it in warm water. Then I cooked it, strained it and added some pulegio (Mentha). Then

I cooked it once more, strained again and put aside. I proceeded the same way with liquiritia; I crushed it, soaked it and cooked it separately; then strained it, again cooked it until it thickened like honey and likewise put aside. Next I took two glasses full of Mentha pulegium infusion, one glass because of the thicker consistency of the liquiritia infusion, one glass of green fennel extract and 2 glasses of thickened grapejuice, mixed everything and dripped it slowly into a pot on a slow fire, all the time skimming the froth arising from the fruit juices, and finally put it down. This yields a magnificent, honeylike elixir pleasing to the palate and, no doubt, of great benefit in this affliction. Then I took the following: Seed of Urtica urens, 3 ounces, stones of pine, soaked and washed, roasted linseed, one ounce each; root of Lilium candidum, Aristolochia longa and Aristolochia rotunda, Inula helenium, Radix valerian, seed of Raphanus sativus, Rubia tinctorum and marrubium half an ounce each; scolopendrium and cumin (Seseli tortuosum) 10 zuzim each; Curcuma 2 zuzim, myrrh 3 zuzim; 13[95] drugs altogether with a total weight of about 17 ounces. I crushed and sifted the mass as much as possible but took care to pulverize the seed and stones until they looked like marrow. The whole mass I kneaded over a slow fire in 14[96] liters of the above mentioned medicine of honeylike consistency. No mention of this preparation is made in any of the books written by either ancient or modern physicians. It is based on logical (scientific) considerations.

I already told Your Highness what actual success I achieved with it. I advise Your Highness to have this preparation always ready and partake of it both in health and on days marked by attacks unless, God forbid, you are laid up with fever.

6. We have already alluded to the fact that the soup of

old chicken assists in the stirring up and ejection of pulmonary phlegm. Ibn Zohar, in referring to the various medicines, which fortify the brain in this disease prefers the powders to the oily pastes. I likewise have told Your Highness that excessive warmth is undesirable in this disorder, which holds good also with regard to cold. I am in a position to recommend the following powder:[97] Valeriana celtica, sandalwood, 2 zuzim each; myrrh, 1 shekel and old camphor a quarter of a zuz, all finely ground, sifted, and kneaded with rose extract to form an electuary. Then the paste is pulverized and applied to a spot devoid of hair (on head?). On hot days this should be mixed with rose extract, on cold ones the top of the head should be massaged with quince oil and sprinkled with the above powder. Quince oil is prepared as follows: take fragrant rose oil, add juice of a quince and half a zuz of mastix, a quarter of a zuz santalum[98] spread over hot cinders until the moisture evaporates and the oil stays behind available for use. It is noteworthy that amber (storax) acts well on a cold and warm brain alike. I also gathered from my teachers, who were much experienced in it, what is, besides, generally known that cichorium (endivia) is very good both for cold and warm liver. Therefore I advise Your Highness always to use this perfume, especially for fumigation, since it purges the brain and prevents it from absorbing or producing residue of any kind. Still another remedy: Take 4 zuzim of ben-nut oil (myrobalanum) uncolored and with no drugs added, dissolve in it 1 shekel of crude amber and Indian santalum album; half a shekel of pressed and filtered oil;[99] a quarter zuz of old camphor—make it up into an ointment[100] and apply to the top of the head and to the face[101] half an hour before leaving the bath. This Your Highness should do on cold days, on warm days take less than usual. At the

time of onset this procedure should be stopped altogether. Modern doctors credit[102] it with the power to
fortify the brain, to dry up superfluous juices and prevent them from moving to other organs. Some of this
perfume[103] may be put on fire and the resultant vapors
inhaled—a highly effective and tested remedy. Another
perfume:[104] Take equal parts of costus, liquidambar,
fresh anise, red orpiment (auripigment), gum resin,[105]
incense (lebonah), galvanum (resin of Ferula galbani-
flua), and mastix. Mix everything and put on fire until
vapors arise, then inhale vapors through nostrils and
mouth until the head and chest are full of them. This
is highly effective. Still another combination is crushed
auripigment and Aristolochia longa mixed with ox fat.
Inhale over a fire.

7. Regarding enemas, here is the mildest of them: cook
half a liter of beet (mangold) water with four ounces of
sesame oil and add 1 zuz of natron. Next in potency:
Boil some oil in wine, add handful of natron or borax,
half a liter of beet juice and 1 liter of fine oil. When
boiled add a bit of natron and the enema is ready.

7a. Next in potency is the following: Anethum, Mentha
silvestris and saturei,[106] about a handful of each, boiled
in water with added fine oil (2 ounces), honey and
Cassia fistula; to be administered when tepid. In case
of marked flatulence add half an ounce of caraway seed.
Duck or chicken fat should be added to the oil in all
the enemas listed so far.

7b. The following is a still better and stronger enema:
To half a zuz coloquinthe is added to the above
ingredients and brought to the boil. If the above is
enriched with camomile,[107] millet[108] (Pannicum milia-
ceum) and Gundabadustur (desiccated substance of

castor fiber glands), the effect is much heightened. These warm enemas should not be administered on hot days, nor when in fever. Only people with singularly thick juices or those suffering from acute constipation should make use of them.

8. Galen cautions against the administration of warm enemas to old people at any time. Strong enemas sometimes give rise to accidents[109] attending strong purgatives and should be abstained from unless it is done on skilled medical advice; moreover, the physician in question should be in attendance and not be content with giving advice[110] from afar.

8a. Of purgatives the following may be mentioned. First, a remedy good for the ejection of phlegm and the clearing of the head: Hiera picra (a ready-made mixture) 1 shekel; agaricum (Fungus laricis) and Turbid half a zuz each; ginger, a quarter zuz. Take a spoonful in julep. Another which is stronger and clears the lungs is Agaricon, half a shekel; Aristolochia, half a zuz; anise, a quarter zuz. A stronger one, for the lungs: Opoponax a half shekel; Hiera picra 1 zuz; coloquinthe a quarter zuz, made up with an equal quantity of pistachio seed and tragacanth resin (astragalus)[111] for drinking.[112]

8b. Another stronger one, of a particularly striking combination, which Your Highness may use as a purgative at stated intervals and during a strong attack: Agaricon and Turbid, half a zuz of each; Hiera picra, 1 zuz; myrrh and root of Lilium candidum and Marrubium, a quarter zuz of each; sarcocoll (Astragalus) one quarter zuz; anise and coloquinthe, aspalathus,[113] blue bdellium, one-eighth shekel of each and all kneaded in grapejuice.

8c. Next in potency: Turpethum, agaricon, cucumber juice[114] (Ecballium elaterium) and absinthe, 1 shekel each; Hiera picra 1 zuz; coloquinthe and astragalus gummifer, one quarter zuz of each;[115] all kneaded in fennelwater and made up with nut oil into pills.

8d. Another stronger one, which clears the lungs wonderfully is this: Coloquinthe and Astragalus gummifer, an eighth shekel of each; anisum, epithymus (Cuscuta epithymum), Ferula sagapenum and Aristolochia, half a shekel of each, kneaded in honeywater. Still another, more potent: Seed of Urtica urens and Polypodium vulgare, 1 zuz of each; coloquinthe juice.[116] And another: Coloquinthe, one quarter zuz; Astragalus gummifer, Bdellium judaicum, a quarter zuz each, three pistachio stones, kneaded in celery water (Apium graveolens) and made up with nut oil in the form of pills. This draws out from the organism the mass of thick, sticky and superfluous juices. Note: All these purgatives are useful in the disease under consideration. However, milder combinations, too, may safely be administered, such as Cassis fistula, myrobolane or rhubarb when the object is to purge the intestinet alone. The latter remedies, to be sure have no effecs whatever on either head or lungs.

9. Below is a list of purgative formulas endorsed by the best physicians in the West and which we have often found of great use ourselves. Their combination is as follows: Agaricon, slit over a sieve for perfect sifting; turbid, peeled at the top, squeezed and sifted, likewise Hiera picra. Coloquinthe, hashed to fine pieces, using only its white part, found in mature, big fruit. Beware of rotten turbid. Any medicine containing coloquinthe or coloquinthe leaves should be prepared in the following manner: Crush the stalk and add the coloquinthe or its cut up leaves, crush pistachio stones after shelling

them with the knife and mix together. Then fetch astragalus from the sifting cloth, add to it coloquinthe and accessories, pound together until it looks like a flat cake. To this are added Hiera picra and the remaining drugs sifted as above. The scammonia and mastix should not be ground too fine.

9a. All other laxative drugs, excepting the ones mentioned above, may be the size of barley, i.e., ground coarse and not sifted, especially the myrobolane which should not be sifted at all but preserved in its natural roughness. All of this is kneaded with some drink into pills dipped in almond oil. If the rest of the organism is to be cleansed also the pills should be small in size and moist. They should be taken early in the morning. In case of pain or spasm boil 3 zuzim bouglosson; stoechus (lavendula), one shekel; ethrog (Satureia hortensis)[117] coloquinthe, each half a zuz. Gulp it down or strain with sugar and drink. This mitigates the pain without affecting in any way the working of the purgatives.

10. All these formulas I received from Western (Moroccan) Masters. Only little thereof is described in books and these too are practically unknown. I listed them here so that all people could make the best use of them. The effect of the purgatives or of their discontinuation, or the treatment of the individual cases which may arise on their application, although an important factor in the overall cure, is certainly outside the province of this book. And this is because this factor is a variable element changing with the kind of medicine used, age, constitution, climate and season of the year.

10a. As for emetics, if used at all, a start should be made with radish, followed up by 2 zuzim of borax and half a liter of honey water. Another stronger emetic: Some slices of white hellebores and solid parts mixed with radish, followed up with honey water. Still another: Sinapis, bolus alba (aromatic borax) and table salt, half a zuz each, natron 2 daniq, dissolve in 3 ounces of water and 1 ounce of honey and drink and vomit.

11. Obviously, the object of the present book is not to cite all the therapeutic measures advisable in the disease under consideration but to mention only those easily available or procurable. With this I believe I have fully acquitted myself and answered the question Your Highness was kind enough to ask me.

XIII

*A Few Paragraphs Which Any Man May Find Useful
with Regard to General Hygiene and Therapy*

THESE ARE to me, not unlike a legacy in their value.[118]
1. THE FIRST thing to consider in this respect is the
provision of fresh air, clean water, and a healthy
diet. Next comes that which the physicians call spiritus,
namely fine vapors found in the living organism of
both man and beast. They derive their origin and
essential part from the air inhaled from the outside.
The Pneuma circulating in the blood of the liver is
called spiritus naturalis, while that found in the heart
and arteries is called spiritus vitalis; the pneuma resid-
ing in the ventricles of the brain and despatched from
there to the various nerves is named spiritus animalis.
Now all these pneumata have a common origin and
this is the air inhaled from the outside. Where such
air is bad or filthy the pneumata change at once and
work to the contrary.

2. Says Galen: Taking care of cleanliness of the surrounding air which enters the body is no less important
than watching any other matter which is exposed to
corruption by contact.*

---

* Inquit Galenus: "Consideratio in substantia aeris quam
contrahit homo in sua aspiratione, est ut sit in fine (sine?)
temperantia(e) ab omni re quae ipsum coinquinat." The sentence is not clear and its Latin translation is not any better.

3. Says the Author: The more delicate the pneuma the more liable is it to be affected by the surrounding air. Thus the spiritus naturalis is (relatively) denser than the vitalis and the latter denser than the animalis.

3a. With any change of the surrounding air the spiritus animalis is altered accordingly. This is why many people, when faced with a sudden climatic disturbance, experience a corresponding upset of their "animal" functions, a kind of stupor,[119] loss of reasoning faculty,[120] or of memory, while their "natural" and "vital" spirits remain unaffected.

4. The relation between the air in a town and in its streets and that found in the open country[121] may be compared to the relation between grossly contaminated, filthy water and its clear, lucid counterpart. Town air is stagnant, turbid and "thick," the natural result of its big buildings, narrow streets, the refuse of its inhabitants, their corpses and animal carcasses, food gone bad and the like. This air the winds carry stealthily inside the houses and many a man become ill even without noticing it. However, when escape seems impossible after one has grown up in the city and become used to its ways, one should at least choose for a residence a wide-open site, facing the north-east, preferably on a steep, wooded mountainside and far from ponds and marshes (for fear of mosquitoes). Should it be impossible to move to another town, a suburb residence, to the south or north, is the next best thing. Living quarters are best located on an upper floor, giving on a wide street exposed to the north wind (for Egypt) and ample sunshine, since sunshine dispels bad air and renders it fine and clear. Toilets should be located as far as possible from living rooms. The air should be kept dry at all times by sweet scents, fumigation and

74

drying agents. The concern for clean air is the foremost rule in preserving the health of one's body and soul.

5. However, even with the greatest care and observance of all the rules some trouble is bound to come; things will happen which are wholly unpredicatable. Thus, e.g., one day one's stool becomes hardened, the next it occurs too often, or there is a mild headache, eventually pain in other parts of the body. In such cases prudence is advocated and no medicine taking attempted. We have it on authority of the leading physicians of all times that in such mild cases nature does well without outside help and there is no need to support her with medicines. A normal, healthy conduct of life is quite sufficient; otherwise, once started with the treatment of relatively mild cases, one of two evils is a sure outcome: either a mistake is made and the therapy applied proves to be contrary to the course of nature, thus impeding the cure and aggravating the pain, or the right thing is done and the disorder guided in its normal channels, thereby teaching nature lazy ways and not to exert herself in the absence of external help. This, they say, reminds one of the horseman who taught his horse not to make a step without being told to do so by its[122] master, to keep quiet until he puts it in motion. This applies to a case where, for example, a diarrhea suddenly sets in with no marked effect on the organism, persisting for two or three days with no pain or actual impairment of health. If obstructing medicines are applied and the diarrhea brought to a stop nature is indeed restored to normal. But, on the other hand it may also bring about the suppression of the natural urge to expel what should be expelled so that nature is actually thwarted by such medicine. Held back by external interference nature is stopped in its tracks, its natural functions unhinged, what should be expelled is

75

retained and troubles arise. Sometimes the diarrhea indicates a weakening of one's power to hold back. Should the organ be left in peace it recovers by itself, dries, and regains its normal function. However, when it is helped along with medicines at the time of its weakness it soon becomes a habit with it always to depend on a stimulant from the outside. This explains why it is important not to tamper with any organ and not to worry about it. This rule holds good in all cases where no danger is to be feared.

6. Abu-Nasser Alfarabi (870–950) has made it clear that the art of medicine, not unlike that of seafaring and farming, is often not worth its trouble. For sometimes the doctor goes about his work very efficiently, no error is made either on his or the patient's part, and still no progress is made to justify all the trouble taken. This is accounted for by the fact that medicine alone is not the only factor in a cure but medicine and nature combined. Sometimes nature does not react for reasons partly explained in this book. The same may happen to the farmer; he does everything that is expected of him and the seed brings forth no fruit. Or with the seaman who builds a ship according to the best plan, steers it masterfully, picks the best season to sail in— and the ship is dashed to pieces. This is explained by the fact that the attainment of the goal depends on two factors. No purpose is served when the one is functioning properly and according to the rules while the other fails completely.

7. On closer examination the above statement seems to imply that sometimes the disease may be mild but nature is much stronger than it. In such a case people exert themselves to get rid of the disorder by resorting to what is known to be efficacious in that regard. Thus,

the physician or the patient by banishing the disorder, nullifies the work of nature.[123] This is actually the main use of medicine[124] in all the countries of the world and in all times.

8. In his Aphorisms Al-Razi says as following: When the disease is stronger than the natural resistance of the organism, medicine is of no use. When one's resistance is stronger than the disease, the physician is of no use. When the two factors are balanced, the physician is called in to increase one's natural powers of resistance and assist them to oust the disease.

9. Says the Author: The writings of this luminary of medicine suggest that one can do without physicians much oftener than having recourse to them, when the general run of diseases is considered. This is true even when it is a question of a prominent physician well acquainted with nature and its power, let alone such that throw nature into disorder and deflect it from its normal course.*

10. How often do famous physicians commit grave errors on patients without the latter succumbing to their disease and with them even coming out alive from it. Many times have I seen a strong purgative prescribed for a patient who did not need even a mild one. This resulted in copious loss of blood from below. This be-

---

* This passage is rather obscure and its translation tentative. Its Latin version is likewise not easily understood. It reads as follows:
Ex verbo huius viri perfecti in arte sua etiam sciri potest, quoniam non indigere medico magis est quam indigere ipso cum facta fuerit comparatio in universis aegritudinibus, et hoc quando fuerit ille ordinatus sciens substantare naturam et iuvare ipsam non quod ponat ipsam in confusionem et eam deponat a sua consuetudine et ordine convenienti.

ing repeated several days an acute diarrhea set in with tenesmus, all of which did not prevent the patient from recovering in a few days.

10a. Another time I witnessed a case of bloodletting with a patient suffering from stomach ulcers (called in Arabic: rachina);[125] the attending physician did not know of his ulcer. The poor man fainted away, his strength left him, the disease became protracted and worse. In spite of it he completely recovered, without anybody knowing the reason for it.

10b. People think that doctors' mistakes cause but little harm. They point to cases where grave errors of judgment were committed with the patients escaping death, while others marked by insignificant errors, e.g., in ordering the right dose of some remedy or light drink, resulted in death. But this is not so. The reason for this often lies with propositions unknown to us. Thus people may be observed with arms cut off up to the elbow, or legs up to the knee, with enucleated eyeballs or deep abdominal gashes, who, far from dying, carry on and live as willed by the Creator. On the other hand, people die of the prick of a tiny needle or thorn and its sequels, blood poisoning and death. The same happens, by analogy, with doctors. One commits a gross blunder and the patient comes through while no mention is made of a supposedly slight mistake which may cause the patient a great deal of harm and for all its insignificance even bring about his death. Any one of sound common sense should bear this in mind.

11. It is commonly believed that considering that no harm attends those who indulge in their habitual food and drink, cold or warm baths, there is likewise no cause for alarm when a sick man does exactly the opposite of what he should do in his condition. But

this is not true. Galen pointed out the fact that serving cold water to a sick man hot with fever is very bad for their juices, their temperature soars and they eventually die. On the other hand there are people for whom a gulp of cold water is a real blessing, their stool is loosened, their fever subsides and they recover. To deny these people a drink would surely spell their death. The same applies to feverish patients put in cold water; some recover, some die of it. It is likewise with those having a steam bath which is intended to cleanse the body. Some of the feverish patients benefit by it greatly, while others pay for it with a deterioration of the rotting process, a rise in temperature and, finally, death. The same holds good with regard to food; sometime the withholding of food may bring about a person's recovery, another time it may spell his death.[126] The reason for all this and the propositions tied up with it, as well as the individual factors, have already been described and amply illustrated. It is indeed easy for any intelligent man to quote examples out of books, but their application in practice to the human body[127] is beset with difficulties even where the expert is concerned. To the layman, however, unversed as he is in the fundamentals of this art, such a consideration is of only slight importance.

12. One of El-Razi's Aphorisms reads as follows: Medicine is an art close to one's heart. Only its mean votaries boast of it; the experts alone know how difficult it is.

13. Says the Author: About this saying of Razi Galen wrote a number of books, all serving to emphasize the truth that "the medical art looks easy and trifling to men of limited horizon but how profound and far-reaching was this art in the eyes of a man like Hippocrates."

13a. However, do not think, dear reader, that this is true of medicine alone. Indeed, turn your eyes to the natural sciences, to mathematics[128] and law[129] and you will see the same. The more a man is proficient in a given discipline the more he thinks of it, the greater his doubts and the more weighty the problems he has to tackle. There is no end to the ideas and thoughts that surge in him and he can scarcely cope with them. On the other hand, to a man of little learning all the weighty problems seem easy to explain, all the remote things within reach, and so great is his conceit that he is prepared to come up with a ready answer at any time and to explain things he does not grasp at all. To come back to what I said before regarding the ease of learning the art of medicine on the part of people with moderate intelligence as against the hazards besetting its practical application, I shall quote the following dictum of Galen:

14. Our advice to massage the old with oil is more easily said than done. It sounds easy when described but is exceptionally difficult when one sets about doing it in practice.

15. Says the Author: Now, consider well, all you people who think honestly: If a mere massaging with oil is classed by Galen as difficult in actual practice, if the matter of water and the abstention therefrom is such as we explained before, how much more serious is the actual performance of blood-letting or the purging with the pith of coloquinthe or with the juice of Cucumis agrestis or helleborus varieties,* eventually with enemas of castor oil and opoponax, cauterization, or plain incision. With the true physician it is never easy and always a matter of serious reflection.

---

* The Hebrew translation differs here from the Arabic original.

80

16. Ibn Zohr in one of his well known extant books, says as follows: "To show you how important it is that you make serious study of the words herein I am going to quote Galen's sayings and commentary word by word so that you keep them always before your eyes and drink in the words to become a part of you: My remarks will follow in due course to explain what is meant by it.

17. "Says Hippocrates: Two things should be borne in mind, one, to help the patient, the other not to harm him.*

18. "Concerning this Galen says: There was a time when I considered this to be superfluous and unworthy of Hippocrates even to mention it. I did it on the assumption that, surely, there was no man who doubted it in the least that all a doctor thinks and cares for is to help his patient and, when unable to do so, at least not to cause him any harm. This question[130] I remember once being discussed by students of medicine, before I entered the medical profession, eventually at the time I used to attend the sick in company with others. Thus I happened to observe that many a prominent practitioner surely deserved censure for having caused harm to many people in that they bled the patients, allowed them to bathe, prescribed them drugged beverages and permitted them to drink wine and ice-cold water. It occurred to me that Hippocrates himself probably witnessed the like, since I do not doubt for a moment that this was the regular procedure with most of his contemporaries. Keeping this in mind I decided from then on to take particular care whenever I thought it advisable to order a patient a stronger diet. First I deliberated with myself what effect this measure

* Hippocrates says: Any time I had to prepare a purgative my heart was beset by it for days before and after.

was liable to yield, eventually what harm it might produce should I err in my diagnosis. In such cases I simply did nothing until I was completely sure that my decision was in no way prejudicial to the patient."

19. To this the Author adds: You, who study this book, would do well to ponder the fact that even great and famous physicians, contemporaries of Galen, sometimes made serious mistakes, if only by allowing the patient to drink cold water or to take a bath, where such things were indeed harmful in their condition, and even Hippocrates himself was not free of it. This is why he was at such pains to guard against trifling with this matter. And Galen, his great experience notwithstanding, relates of himself that whenever he was faced with the problem of prescribing a remedy for a sick man he never relied on his own opinion and understanding nor listened to the voice of his own reasoning, but argued with himself on such lines: Theoretically speaking this drug is sure to banish the affected juice (humour);[131] but the question arises whether such ejection is good in itself and if the development would be as anticipated, further, if the patient would not suffer any harm should he proceed with just the opposite of what he decided. Only then did he order the relevant potion. However, when he found out that applying the opposite of what he decided caused the patient great harm, he was not slow in throwing his opinion and its logical implications to the four winds. Such was his attitude also with regard to blood-letting and the other prescriptions he enumerates. Considering that even Galen, with his vast knowledge and long medical practice, his devotion to the art, his diligence and thoroughness, could not help entertaining doubts in medical matters and going back on his decisions,

how truly appropriate is doubt in the case of doctors who are relative newcomers in this profession which requires experience so long that a man's lifetime is hardly sufficient to cover a part, let alone the whole art of medicine, as I have explained in my Commentary to the Aphorisms of Hippocrates. I have indeed enlarged upon this point to make it clear to Your Highness to beware of "certain" physicians and not to put your life in the hands of any of them just because he happens to be there, but to rely at all times on a healthful way of life whose principles we have discussed here. The main thing you may have learned from this is that erroneous judgment is much more frequent with doctors than is the right procedure.

20. Aristotle, in his treatise[132] on natural sciences, says as follows: The first thing required of a doctor is that he learn the nature of his patient's constitution on both healthy and sick days. Most physicians fail to establish the true facts so that, in the last resort, the doctor and his "remedy" are to blame for the patient's death.

21. Says the Author: On this point another version ascribes to him the following saying: "Most people die of medicine." And I say Aristotle is worth listening to in this respect. And in his days the art of medicine was admittedly at its highest and physicians engaged in it alone to the exclusion of any other calling. I have cited for the benefit of Your Highness only a few relatively unknown but praise-worthy passages from earlier writings to keep you acquainted which what is true and useful in the art of medicine.

22. I can imagine Your Highness saying to yourself: "If this is all your argument leads to, why not leave medi-

cine alone, for surely all the alleged profit there is in it is an empty boast." I am going to relieve you of this uncertainty. Even if it may be implied in the words of my predecessors I shall repeat it here, to wit: It should be clear that medicine is a science essential to man, at any time, anywhere; not only in times of illness but in health as well. It may truly be said that medicine (the medical man) should be a man's constant companion. To be sure, this holds good only in the case of a consummate physician with a complete mastery of theoretical and practical knowledge, so that a man may safely lodge himself in his hands, body and soul, to be guided by his directions. Such phyiscians are encountered[133] in all countries and in all times. On the other hand, if only uncultured (imperfect) physicians are available, who unfortunately comprise the bulk of the profession, it is best not to rely upon them in the same that a man might make shift with bad food when no good food was available. Though he cannot do without food, he can certainly manage without placing his body and soul in the hands of one who has not the slightest notion of science. In such circumstances it is best to entrust his case to the care of nature and rely on her while keeping the relatively best diet according to one's own lights (and conscience). This we have already sufficiently explained, namely that the clever, skilled physician who is versed in the fundamentals of medicine[134] thinks twice before he decides how to bring about a patient's relief, and such a man always relies on the work of nature and keeps her from going lazy, as described above. Such a physician knows what diseases he can forestall and what symptoms he can combat before they get worse and assume proportions he can no longer manage. He knows when there is true cause for fear and alarm and takes pains to

84

caution when necessary to mitigate any danger, as Galen tells about himself. In dubious cases, when the best course is to do nothing, he would deliberate with himself if it were not better to leave medicines alone and wait for nature to take its beneficial course. Even if he does take action he follows nature's example and goes in its footsteps, as taught by Hippocrates and Galen. This is why it is so important to listen to such a physician and adhere strictly to his prescriptions. Even if he errs in any of these things it is only an occasional, rare occurrence. With a poor man (a patient) on his hands he will never waver in his obligation towards him and always call his attention to any danger that may threaten him. On the other hand, the inexperienced physician may go on treating a patient even if he does not understand a thing. Sometimes he succeeds, sometimes he fails. His failures, however, far outnumber his successes which besides, come about by pure chance. Thus, if no skilled physician is to be had a man should leave his case to nature. Sometimes he is lucky, sometimes not.[135] But lucky chances are by far more numerous and reliable and bad luck is rare and incidental. Thus every reasonable man might better rely on nature than on the advice of a medical ignoramus. Unfortunately, most people do not act like this but let themselves be treated by anyone who happens to be at hand, in any emergency. Unfortunately, most of the physicians belong to this category (i.e., not knowing the real nature of their work), confirming Aristotle's saying that most people die of medicines and remedies.

23. Hippocrates says as follows: Nature cures disease. Then nature has a way with it, she takes no orders from man's devices; also nature does everything that should be done because she is superior and endowed

85

with the highest knowledge (ethics); anything we know derives from her, our ethics (morals) come from her.

24. Says the Author: These sayings occur in many of his writings. He teaches people always to follow in nature's footsteps, which are reliable and acknowledged as such by all those who are experienced.

25. Galen says, in one of his famous books, as follows: The Greeks, whenever doubt arose with regard to any disease, always thought it best to rely on nature and her doings which were sure, in the last resort, to banish the disease. They based their opinion on the following grounds: Nature, being the servant and provider of all living things in healthy days, helps them also in disease; she knows best the constitution of the organs, provides each of them with the food it needs, etc., provides for the places and channels whereby residue is discarded and the normal distribution of bodily juices thus assured.

26. Says the Author: On closer scrutiny these words seem to confirm what I have said above, namely when after careful search no skillful physician is found and one is in doubt about the nature of the disease, it is best left to nature (no cure to be undertaken), according to what I have said before.

27. Having heard all this Your Highness should in no way conclude that I am the right man in whose hands you might place your body and soul for treatment. Heaven be my witness that I myself know well that I belong to those who are not perfect in this art (medicine) and shrink from it (for lack of adequate experience), because it is enormously difficult to attain its

end. There is no doubt that I know myself better than anyone else and can match my knowledge with that of all others and of those less learned than I am.[136] Again, heaven be my witness that the words I say are not motivated by any modesty such as pious men resort to when deliberately understating their knowledge even if they are experts in their vocation and making little of their own deeds even when highly diligent and active. I state the truth as it is. I say this only for fear lest, while reading this book, Your Highness might think I wrote it for my own advantage and thus take lightly my advice in the belief that considerations of personal gain might have crept in and thus you might be slack in following my prescriptions. This is the only reason why I enlarge upon it. Now I shall come back to that which I took upon myself to explain.

28. Anyone who has anything to do with medicine, and in fact most people, know that it is an art which relies both on practical experiment and on theoretical reasoning. Practical experience plays by far the greater role. Observing this, people are apt to give preference to the skillful experimenter. This (attitude) took on such proportions that the mass of the people (in western countries) have a standard saying: "Ask the experienced, not the physician." Thus they harmed medicine and made people rely on old women's tales, (attributed) wisdom to anybody who came along and boasted of "experience," so that any scoundrel and self-conceited fool got access to medicine. It was enough for him to say "I have some proven remedies." Soon they collected a number of followers who declared them to be "physicians," partly because they had "experience" and partly because they were old and grey. And so the multitude says of them: Maybe he is no learned phy-

sician but he has "experience" and is well versed in actual treatment. Naturally, this is all nonsense and leads to that which we have already branded above.

29. The root of the trouble is that people believe experience* with curative measures implies the experience of this or that physician. This is not so. It means the experience of all physicians and over many generations, up to the time of Galen and Hippocrates. Their experience is written down in medical books. Some drugs and combined remedies took hundreds of years to evolve and the outcome is enclosed in scientific treatises. But that wretch is certainly shut off from gathering experience if only for lack of preliminary knowledge (to make proper experiments with the various kinds of people and to evaluate results). Even an honest physician would think twice before he admits carrying out such experiments and gathering such experience; even Hippocrates (in his Aphorisms) says experience has its dangers. In our time quacks boast of experience and lead people astray with words which ring alike but have other meanings, all aimed to conceal their ignorance.

30. There is another cause for mistake in that people may acquire practical experience in medicine without (extensive) study. On the other hand it is quite possible and true, that there are medical scholars who are highly proficient in the principles and branches of medicine without having any practical experience in its application, i.e., have studied medicine from books, not from masters of this science, and have never engaged in it in practice. But nobody can be called a good physician who has observed or witnessed some facts without having engaged in their theoretical study. Because medicine is not a craft like carpentry or weav-

---

* Poiré: "Experientia" of Hippocrates, Aph I, 1.

ing which can be acquired by practice. It is gaining perfection by changing circumstances. Training in this art implies most often a combination of practice and theory. Any sick individual presents new problems. One can never say one disease is just like the other.

30a. There is a general rule, and I have seen great physicians acting on it (which is also in keeping with the medicine of Hippocrates and Galen) that the physician should not treat the disease but the patient who is suffering from it.*

30b. However, the precise description of these tasks and aims is not intended in this treatise. What I aim at is that Your Highness should not let himself be cajoled with false promises but always rely on scientifically trained practitioners. Knowledge is the root and practice is the bough and there is no bough without a root behind it, although roots may be found which can as yet boast no boughs, as we explained before. I have also mentioned in this book the man who submits to the treatment of an "experienced" practitioner who has no education but a flair for attending to matters as they come; such a man may be likened to a sailor who may be saved or drowned as pure chance may have it. Of this Galen spoke much and enlarged upon it in his books, meaning experience and experimenters, saying as follows: Knowledge shows a man the direction where he can find what he is looking for. He who experiments without theory (Logic) and knowledge is like the blind man who does not know which way to go.

31. Says the Author: Considering that the experimenter resembles a blind man it may be said that he who

---

* The Latin translation of this important dictum reads: quoniam medicus non curabat speciem aegritudinis sed individuum ipsius.

places himself in his hands may be likened to the sailor, i.e., he may be saved or drown, by chance.

32. What I have said before, that a physician may make a mistake in prescribing (cold) water or precluding some drink, eventually ordering a bath and aggravating thereby a patient's condition, is indeed true, since I cited it after Galen, but it is a relatively rare occurrence. I mentioned it to make absolutely clear that Your Highness should refrain, where strong (dangerous) remedies are concerned, from relying on people who have no sufficient knowledge of medicine. Of all remedies there are none more perilous than blood-letting and purgatives, next come emetics and strong enemas. In this regard one should never rely on chance doctors. Nevertheless you find people, both healthy and sick, who depend on barbers to pronounce on blood-letting and on untried youths to prescribe purgatives. Galen pointed out the fact which has since become a medical maxim, that some people should never be subjected to blood-letting if they do not show symptoms indicating a plethora. Similar regulations exist for purging of the intestines and emetics. It all depends, as explained above, on the kind of disease, on its severity and on the inherent strength (of the patient). He explains what is meant by severity of the disease. He goes on to explain that sometimes symptoms of plethora are found in healthy people, in full vigor, who have no need of blood-letting at all, neither of purgatives nor of emetic, but would often manage, the one with a fast day, the other with curtailed diet, the third with a sweat-bath and still another with a mild laxative. And a mild laxative, to all accounts, is still no purgative. One would do with a steam bath, the other with physical exercise, a third with strong massage, etc., all of which are of great importance. Now, having given sufficient thought to

the matter, decide for yourself if all these things require the services of a skilled physician or may be left to him who learned his medicine from chance observation.

33. To illustrate the point I shall cite the case of a perfectly healthy and well-proportioned young man, whom I met in the West, who fell ill with febris continua.[137] On the second day of the illness his physician administered phlebotomy. Having drained some 50 zuzim (200 grams) of blood the patient felt worse (his spirits fell) and the flustered physician closed the cut at once. He ordered that he be given rose syrup and oxymel, and left undisturbed until next morning and then treated as usual. But the patient died that very night. This gave rise to a discussion between the physician and the people. One of the masters (professors) of medicine with whom I studied (along with the other students), told me as follows: Do you know what mistake that physician made in administering phlebotomy to his patient? "No Sir," said I, "so you too infer a mistake was made?" The master chuckled and said: Well, it seems that patient was a man who liked his food too much.[138] This overeating[139] (blocked and) weakened his pylorus[140] and gave rise to choleric juices in the stomach. In such cases Galen said no phlebotomy should be administered because the patient tends to lose consciousness in the act. The right thing to do* would have been to strengthen the stomach outlet and to treat the patient with some external remedies after the discharge (and only then administer phlebotomy) if all other measures fail. Having decided to let his blood before acting in this manner he should at least have strengthened the pylorus (without delay). Failing to do this[141] the juices spread and aggravated

---

* Extant only in the Latin manuscript and missing in the Hebrew one.

the weakness of the pylorus, the patient fainted and eventually died. Thus spoke my esteemed teacher.

34. Says the Author: Just consider, how many doubts (dangers) may attend such cases. This is why I advise Your Highness not to put trust in any chance practitioner. In this respect I think it worthwhile to cite a saying of Galen according to which he once ordered phlebotomy to a man with febris continua and let the blood flow uninterruptedly until the patient lost consciousness. However, he qualified this by saying that no blood-letting is admissible in febrile cases, let alone in diseases of a graver nature. These include also surfeit of the stomach (vomiting, nausea, heartburn), pain in the pit of the stomach, accompanied by singultus, loss of strength, then old age, a weakened constitution, unfavorable climatic conditions and the season. He also says that anybody who produces juices in the neighborhood of the pylorus or whose pylorus is diseased and highly sensitive, should never be given phlebotomy. This he follows up with the statement:

35. Referring to what I said about the advisability of blood-letting to the point of a fainting fit I think it helps in mitigating the heat of the chronic fever, occasioned by the unsettled digestion, and soothing the inflammation. In most cases, however, (blood-letting) causes no small harm, namely when it is administered at the wrong time or in the wrong proportions.

36. I know of two cases in which death occurred after fainting fits occasioned by the intervention of physicians, I am told, after blood-letting. The patients succumbed on the spot. Other cases did not die at once, but after some time, of progressive weakening. On the other hand, febrile cases where blood-letting

stopped short of total invalidation, stayed alive. Again, others suffered long from grave diseases because their strength ebbed away from excessive loss of blood. Others suffered a change in their normal constitution and acquired a life-long cold disposition which no remedy could improve. All this caused by excessive blood-letting. This change of constitution causes in some people a change in appearance or a lowering of their stamina so that they easily fall ill on the slightest occasion. Eventually they become critically asthenic, their liver and stomach functioning fails them (hydropsy), some fall into lethargy, suffer loss of strength and show paralytic symptoms.

37. Says the Author: Just consider what harm there is in blood-letting, generally inadvisable and of particular consequence when indulged in to excess. Consequently it vindicates my advice to Your Highness not to put yourself hastily under care of some chance doctor. And what is said of blood-letting, says Galen, is equally true of other kinds of bodily discharges when they occur in the wrong time (or in excessive quantities).

38. Medicines such as theriac (al-farouk), mithridate, theodorites and the like, concocted from numerous drugs and held in high esteem by doctors, have a powerful effect similar to that of the above-mentioned remedies. They should not be resorted to in any case, particularly by sick people, before consulting a physician. All these medicines, when taken in the right time and in prescribed cases, are useful in warding away (curing) many grave and dangerous diseases. However, if an error is committed in diagnosis and prescription or they are administered out of time and in wrong doses, the patient may either perish or suffer severe pain.

38a. In times past, in Morocco, the following came to pass: It has to do with the Sultan Amrael-Muselmin (Latin MS: Hachin, dominus Saracenorum). One day he fell ill. I never learned with what disease. He was about 20 years old and of powerful build. The time (he fell ill) was winter, the town the capital city of the Moroccan kings, Marakesh. He recovered from his illness but was not yet in his full vigour, merely in a convalescent condition. The physicians treated him with a diet common in convalescent cases. Among them were four of the greatest professors of medicine: Abu 'Ali Ibn Zohar,[142] Se(ra)pion, Abu -Elchassan ben Qamniel of Saragossa, the Jew, and Abu -Ayub ben Elmu'alim of Sevilla, the Jew. Since they found no defect in his organism, only that he was not fully recovered and had a weak digestion and little natural warmth, and since he drank no wine (being a Muslim) the four physicians decided to prescribe him half a zuz (2 grams) of the great theriac to stir up his warmth (blood circulation), strengthen his digestion and restore all his bodily functions to their right proportions, which is exactly the effect the great theriac is known to have. They all agreed to administer it to him at the end of the third watch of the night, so[143] that it would not mix with the food, this being a prime condition. (Having thus made up their minds) the physicians that night went to sleep in the royal palace. When the time came they administered the dose agreed upon brought sealed from the Royal pharmacy. Early in the morning they again came to the patient's place, to the palace, to discuss what food he should have.[144] That was the third or fourth hour before the morning prayer. All of a sudden the palace rang with a terrible scream. The people rushed for the physicians but the Sultan died just as they came in or a few seconds after. I was told by Abu Yussuf the physician, on the author-

94

ity of his father, the above named Abu Ayub, that the mistake lay in the dosage, i.e., he could take only a quarter of a zuz (1 gram) or a quarter aureus (shekel). I was subsequently told by the minister, Abu Bekr ibn Abi-Merwan ibn Abi El 'Ali that his father[144a] Abu Merwan (ibn Zohar) . . . thought that (his above named son) Abu'Ali made a mistake in the dose of the theriac. He maintained death occurred because of an insufficient dose. He should have taken only half an aureus (shekel). The real cause I did not learn from any of the physicians, whether a too large or a too small dose was to blame for the outcome. I made individual investigations (on psychological grounds) with a view to promoting medical science and help (ailing humanity).[145]

39. Quite a time passed, having studied this and that (of medicine), when I found in Galen the following words which I faithfully repeat here. He said: All medicines, antidotes by nature, when taken in excessive doses cause the organism the greatest harm. Therefore it is necessary that their prescribed quantity fall always short of the maximum dose which might harm the body (but not be too weak, because of a mild dose, to remove dangerous defects).[146]

40. Says the Author: I suppose those physicians who offered an explanation of that case seemed to imply regret at not consulting, in that matter, the writings of some classical author.[147] I have heard a great many other arguments in that case but it is of no use to enlarge upon them here. I hope with this to have achieved my aim and put my patients on guard not to be reckless with strong medicines but to resort to them only on the advice of a reliable, eminent physician and even then with great circumspection and when there is no other way.

95

41. The procedure of the Egyptians with regard to curative drugs of the materia medica, if one may at all speak in this respect of a materia medica, is somewhat as follows: They keep their patients on a diet only to put them on their feet by the power of nature and (when this power fails) they simply let them die. Generally speaking this is a laudable method and I agree with it on various grounds, I would like to describe this method in detail and point out the reasons why I find it praiseworthy. What struck me about their methods is that they are extremely cautious, so much so that most of the single and combined remedies (used by doctors all over the world) fell with them in desuetude. Thus, they rely on a relatively small number of drugs for regular use.[148] When they have to dilute or bring to the boil some diseased thick juice they resort to weak drugs which attain only the first degree of temperature, occasionally the second. The utmost they use for purging is Cassia fistula, rhubarb, agaricon and myrobalan, of the "hierae" (combined, strong laxatives) none more potent than Hiera picra. Most of their combined medicines consist of vegetabilia such as apple juice, common flowering plants and fruit drinks, which go by the name of "Rub." Only rarely do they prescribe composita of many-sided effects whether theriacs or electuaria, known as "Rebid." Occasionally, when they add something according to need and taste, say some roses, they call it rose-electuarium (diarrhodon). They never use a strong purgative liquid. Such is their method. I said already I hold it in high esteem, this for four reasons:

42 The first and most important is the one we have already mentioned in this connection, the shortage of physicians who command sufficient knowledge in these arts. When he uses a mild remedy the doctor is in most

cases successful. When he errs and follows the wrong course the patient does not necessarily die, at the most he may have his illness protracted a bit longer.[149]

43 The second reason is this: The country is hot; Egypt lies in the subtropic zone. This is a natural condition and will not take up much of our time here. The climate weakens and no strong remedies should be used in hot countries or for an enfeebled organism. This might have brought about the death of the king[150] who died from a theriac while convalescing, since potent remedies tend to undermine a man's strength. When the strength is already reduced and wasting away to such an extent that it cannot be restored to its former condition, (the poison) is all the more able to overcome it.

44. The third reason is that most of the (Egyptians') diseases are of an acute character, attributable to the delicacy of juices and their lean bodies. Such diseases do not respond to strong medicine. It is well known that acute cases were treated by Hippocrates and Galen only with sekang'bin (oxymel), barley porridge, and the like.[151]

45. The fourth reason is that they actually follow the rule laid down by the great masters of medicine. This is that anything that might be cured with food (diet) should not be treated by any other means. When this fails[152] mild drugs should be used and anything which might be cured with simple remedies should not be treated with combined remedies, and even then only the least complicated should be used. If successful, everything one aimed at has been achieved. The truth of this has been acknowledged by the greatest physicians. Such is the procedure adopted by the Egyptians

in most cases. No doubt, grave diseases may occur which require stronger medicines. In such cases they do in fact lag behind because they have never experimented with potent remedies. At any rate, their remedies generally cause no harm and their good points outweigh the bad ones.

46. The remarkable thing about them, however, is that they are afraid to use the four-fold theriac (containing four ingredients) and similar highly useful remedies, some pomegranate electuria[153] (ciminum), or mentastrum[154] and other health promoting medicines; on the other hand they resort to repeated blood-letting, entailing much loss of blood and prescribe often[155] purging drugs as a matter of regular hygiene, even for old people. All this is, of course, patently wrong and deserving of the utmost attention.

47. Another thing I learned in Egypt is that it seldom happens, with prominent families or with the common people, that the one and the same physician should treat a patient from beginning to end. In most cases they run from doctor to doctor (to consult him), sometimes a patient, if able to afford it, is treated simultaneously by ten doctors not knowing about each other. Thus the patient leads the doctor astray by telling him he does everything ordered. The patient or the person in charge of him listens to what each doctor has to say, decides who is right and takes the medicines which he decides are the best. But the worst thing is the confusion of the patient himself who can hardly know which physician is right. When he decides in favor of one of them he is plagued by doubt thinking that the other may be right.

47a. Another cause for trouble is the doctor's confusion. Since, when conducting his treatment from beginning to end he is in a position to stick to a method which has proved successful or to adopt another method when the opposite is true.

47b. The third risk lies in the mutual incrimination of the doctors. Each one of them speaks ill of his colleagues and put the blame on them. The fourth risk lies in the (doctor's) indifference (to the case) and his reliance on others, reasoning thus: in case of faulty treatment he would not be the only one to be called to account, and if successful not the only one to be credited. Therefore he would not take great pains to guide the patient according to his best knowledge because he knows other doctors would also be consulted.

48. Says El Razi: He who lets himself be treated by many physicians is never sure if they all made no mistake.

49. Says the Author: This is true when all of them treat him separately. However, when they are gathered together, in consilium as is the case with kings and wealthy families, comparing their observations and deliberating on the best course to be taken, it is highly advisable and becoming. The patient has the benefit of the sum of their knowledge and ability, since no man can remember everything he learns and this art is not easy for its votaries, especially where memory is concerned, which has nothing to do with intelligence.[156] It may well happen that a physician should not be able to muster on the spot everything he might require for his patient.

49a. However, when several come together, they remind and assist each other to arrive at the desired end and so the best medical treatment is assured by use of the collegium.

49b. If they quarrel with each other and each one of them wants to come out victorious and show off before his patient his excellence in this science and the alleged ignorance of his colleague it is a danger signal and they should all be left alone, otherwise it will be the end of the patient who follows the advice of the victor. From (physicians) afflicted with this "malady,"[157] only evil can be expected because decency has been thrown to the winds, even if it is a case of a perfect master of medicine. Therefore my advice in cases like these is to get rid of all of them and rely on the work of nature alone. Our sages[158] once said: Love and hate (emotions) lead (heavenly) judgment[159] astray.

50. Says Alexander Aphrodisius: The causes underlying a quarrel are threefold: First, the pursuit of fame and victory, which prevents people from seeing things as they really are; second, the inherent profundity and refinement of ideas which are not easily communicable to others(?) ; third, inability to comprehend the comprehensible.

51. Says the Author: I would like to add a fourth cause to those enumerated by Alexander. It may well be assumed that he failed to mention it because it was either non-existent in his times or present only in a small degree. This is the force of habit, the tendency to cling to preconceived ideas, the inertia of one's acquired habits, irrespective of whether they are things or ideas. Man is inclined to profess those opinions in which he was reared and which became a habit with him, a second nature. Another point of view is abhorrent to him even if it surpasses his own in accuracy. Thus, for example, he prefers bad food to a wholesome but strange diet. However, this is outside the scope of the present treatise. What I intended was to bring out in

greater clarity the first reason Alexander gave for quarrelling and support it from a philosophical point of view. This concludes the present chapter, wherein I have cautioned against a great many errors incidental to hygiene and the treatment of the sick.

May God the Gracious and the Truthful guide us on the right way to our salvation in eternity. Praise be to God for ever and ever.

Note: The conclusion of the Arabic manuscript reads as follows: "Copy by the son of excellent ability Abu 'Imram Musa ben 'Ubaidallah" (i.e., Maimonides).

NOTES

1. In Arabic Ms. and seen by myself.
2. Arabic: This asthma.
3. From which thick and sticky mixtures originate.
4. Arabic: Brain.
5. Arabic: It does the chest no good.
6. In Arabic MS: Isfidabadj, prepared from red beet, chicken or mutton.
7. Arabic: Zabibiya.
8. In Arabic: No lauz (almonds), laun (dishes).
9. Arabic: Mentha.
10. Arabic: Qirfaz, cinnamon, and Karawiyya, caraway seed.
11. Arabic: Muscat blossom.
12. In Arabic: Tanbul, also betel leaves.
13. Arabic: Nasha: starch (amylum).
14. Sentence missing in Arabic text.
14a. Medical science, as is well known, exists for the benefit of Homo sapiens and every man should know his proper food intake on normal days.
15. Literally, to let the food sink from the stomach.
16. Arabic: Khamr, anbidha (pl. from nbidh) anathema to most people.
17. Arabic: Shows a highest degree of excellence and based on theoretical reasoning.
18. Conclusion missing in Arabic Ms.
19. Stalks.
20. Age.
21. In Arabic: Drawn on the same day from running water.
22. Originally, mastix.
23. Alleviates thirst.
24. Literally: . . . assists digestion and causes the food to be held tightly by the stomach walls.
25. Original: dropsy (ascites).
26. Original: colds, nazalath.
27. Arabic: And a purgative must be taken.
28. Arabic: Chinese rhubarb.
29. Arabic: Qurtum.
30. Arabic: Lubab saghir (cornel, cornouiller).

31. Arabic: Of which half a liter.
32. Arabic: terebinth resin, samgh el butm.
33. First one then the other should be taken.
34. So long as its warmth is retained.
34a. Sebesten.
35. Arabic: With licorice roots and marsh mallow (khitmi, Althaea officinalis).
36. Mahmuda.
37. Arabic: The excellent.
38. Arabic: Galen mentions a number (mispar, not besefer) of enemas.
39. In Arabic: "Red beet" instead of beet.
40. Arabic: Can be effected quite easily.
41. The ancient physicians.
42. Arabic: Salted fish.
43. In Arabic Ms. Or other remedies by which the stomach is flooded, disrupting and carrying away the phlegm, when there are no juices sticking to the stomach walls . . .
44. Let Your Highness proceed as you are used to . . . .
45. White radish.
46. Arabic: Or three.
47. Arabic: One fills the belly with it then waits a while until the replete stomach is stirred into action, then his eyes are covered and the belly tied up below the stomach, after which the prescribed liquid is taken in lukewarm condition.
48. Arabic: Zirbag, mixture of sugar, almonds, vinegar,
49. Bulbus maritima.
50. Arabic: A great offense.
50a. According to the original text it may be translated: "but gradually until nature supports it and would be out-witted and would steal into itself."
51. Arabic: Prohibited (by the physicians).
52. Arabic: A bath should be taken only on an empty stomach.
53. Arabic: After leaving.
54. Arabic: Baths.
55. Arabic: Later physicians say that the right limit is when a bath is taken not oftener than once in every ten days.
56. Arabic: This concludes all the useful things to be said with regard to a man's habits.

57. The Arabic MS adds: the current point of view does not endorse all the kinds of massage recommended by Galen.

58. Arabic: The pains occasionally appearing in some organs can be stopped from recurring by this kind of massage.

59. Massaging the chest during an attack is highly dangerous, it should be performed in between attacks or two hours before an attack.

60. Arabic: And internal warmth.

61. Arabic: Decline of mental power.

62. Also not before several days elapsed after the blood-letting.

63. Purgatives.

64. Arabic: He collapsed in the evening.

65. For the general cleanliness of the body.

66. Any organ free of residue, which is the case here, and enjoying its natural temperament, is considered healthy unless it is attacked by disease.

67. In Arabic also: Only the thin juices dissolve, while the turbid ones solidify.

68. Arabic: Hot and thin, chārā-chādā.

69. Arabic: Everything mentioned in the books treats of disease in general, not any special kind of disease. These kinds, to be sure, vary greatly with the varying kinds of people.

70. Alternative rendering: you should start with the least diluted and take the lightest food.

71. And if it does you good, then . . . .

72. At set seasons.

73. Arabic: When the attack reaches its peak.

74. For the various kinds of this disease.

75. According to the plan of the present book.

76. Arabic: Kuzbarat bir, Adiantum capillus veneris.

77. Arabic: Kuzbarat bir.

78. Arabic here: 'Irq sus- Glycyrrhiza.

79. Kuzbarat bir.

80. Arabic: Druggists, 'attarun.

81. Qanturiyun, Erythraea centaurium Pers. (not in Hebrew Ms.).

82. Arabic: Asl susan, susan roots.

83. Arabic: Qanturiyun s.o.

84. Kuzbarat bir.

85. Qiththa (Maimonides, Drugs, 327)
86. 'Unab, fruit of several ziziphus varieties (Maimonides, Drugs, 291)
87. In some concoction of manna (taranjubin).
88. 'Irq sus.
89. Arabic: Instead of fanid I have used here syrup of quince-lemon (limu-safarjali, grapefruit?) as well as the liquid of cooked Adiantum capillus veneris with almond oil.
90. Hashchash.
91. Arabic: Fresh, white.
92. Arabic: Spare flow.
93. Arabic: The flow of phlegm stops and nothing is left but what is in the lung.
94. Nasha.
94a. Arabic: she was still unmarried.
95. Arabic: 18.
96. Arabic: 4 liters.
97. Arabic: Muscat blossom, 3 zuzim.
98. Arabic: Sunbul (valieriana)
99. "Oil" missing in Arabic text.
100. Arabic: Concoction.
101. Arabic: Forehead.
102. Arabic: Fumigants.
103. Arabic: Here belongs the cactus which they (the physicians) say should be kept on fire.
104. Fumigant.
105. Resin of terebinth, samgh el butm.
106. Arabic: Qanturiyun.
107. Arabic: Sakabing, sagapenum.
108. Arabic: G 'awashir, opoponax.
109. On negligent application.
110. Gives orders.
111. Arabic: Kathira.
112. Arabic: Has it "with honey water."
113. Arabic: Kathira
114. Arabic: Juice of absinthe.
115. Arabic: Also: Convolvulus scammonia and mastix, from each 1/8 zuz; of blue bdellium, half a zuz.
116. Arabic: Alqam, wild cucumber, also: coloquinthe, 1/4 zuz.
117. Ysop, food.
118. Penetrating warning.

119. Stultification.
120. Ability to comprehend.
121. To the air of deserts and wide open fields (Forests).
122. Arabic: Poking stick.
123. Arabic: Either the physician errs in his treatment or the patient makes some mistake, both resulting in the obliteration of the part played by nature.
124. This happens most.
125. Should read in Arabic: Tukhma, stomach ache.
126. In Arabic also: The preparation of food, too, may be the cause of either recovery or death.
127. In a given case.
128. Arabic: Humanities.
129. Arabic: Religious science.
130. Such was my opinion when I began studying medicine, before I went into practice myself or was even allowed to attend at the practice of others.
131. In such a case and the symptoms being as they were a certain juice responded to a certain drug.
132. Arabic: In one of his famous books.
133. But such a man is a rare phenomenon.
134. And scientifically trained, knowing which diseases should not be tampered with but left in the hands of nature.
135. Nature, sometimes she succeeds, sometimes fails.
136. Arabic: And that I am in a position to judge and evaluate my own knowledge and that of others much better than the one lagging behind me in scientific insight.
137. So in Arabic text.
138. Arabic also: Although he had severe pain in the stomach.
139. Arabic: This boil.
140. Arabic: It weakened the pylorus to such an extent that it lost its functioning power.
141. Arabic: But he became alarmed, left and . . . .
142. Avenzoar's father, who died in 1131.
143. Arabic: At the third hour of the day, when he took his meal and the theriac had already left his stomach having been assimilated.
144. Arabic: Then they returned to their place in the palace, intending to visit their patient at the agreed morning hour. However, when three hours passed,

just before the morning prayer set in, a terrible cry was heard. . .

144a. Has to be read: "his grandfather."
145. Here the Arabic MS: intending to be of use (to mankind) and further my own knowledge. But they kept silent and that was that.
146. Extant only in Arabic MS and Latin translation.
147. Arabic . . . implied that in this respect they found some explicit information in classical works, apart from those I cited myself.
148. Arabic: Having a slight effect.
149. In Arabic MS: So long as they (the quacks) operate with mild drugs there is no serious danger. Where they chance upon the right remedy the patient recovers, where they make a mistake the patient keeps alive, the worst that can happen to him is to have his illness prolonged. Drastic remedies, when used out of place, invariably cause death.
150. Arabic: Young man.
151. Sentence missing in Arabic MS.
152. In Arabic also: Then curative foods should be given and when this fails . . .
153. Arabic: Kamun, cumin, caraway.
154. Faudanaj, mentha.
155. In different seasons of the year.
156. Arabic also: For most scholars this science is rather difficult because of the enormous mass of information to be learned, not because it is hard on the intellect.
157. Arabic: So that each of them is forced to call the right thing false and faulty, even if he is perfect in his art.
158. Arabic: Astrologers.
159. Arabic: Judgment (i.e., they judge people in advance). Cf. Sanhedrin 105a and R. Moses ibn Ezra: Love blinds the eye to defects, hate blinds the eye to skill.

INDEX

References are to chapter and numbered section.

Hedgehog, III, 7
Helleborus, XII, 10; XIII, 15
Hemlock, III, 10
Hen, IX, 13
—s'-fat, yolk, III, 4
Herbs, VIII, 1
Herring, IX, 13
Hiera picra, XII, 8, 9; XIII, 41
Hippocrates, I, 3; V, 5; X, 8; XI,
    4; XIII, 13, 17, 18, 19, 22,
    23, 29, 30, 44
Honey, III, 1; V, 4, 5; VI, 5; VII,
    2; IX, 6, 7, 13, 15; XII, 1, 3,
    4, 7, 10
Honey water, IX, 3; XII, 8, 10
Humidity, VIII, 1
Humours, I, 1, 2
Hunger, VI, 3
Hydropsy, XIII, 36
Hyssop, XII, 1

Ibn Zohar, IX, 1
Ibn Zohr, XIII, 16
Ill luck, VIII, 3
Impotence, V, 6; IX, 8, 10
Incense, XII, 6
Indian date, IX, 1
Infection, X, 8
Inflammation, I, 1; V, 6; VII, 4
Infusion, XI, 4; XII, 3, 5
Inhalation, XII, 6
Insomnia, V, 6
Intestinal fat, III, 6
Intestines, IX, 6; XII, 8
Inula helenium, XII, 5

Jaundice, XIII, 33
Jew, XIII, 38
Joints, V, 6; IX, 15
Juices, bad, II, 1; III, 4; V, 3, 4,
    5; VI, 3, 4; IX, 1, 8, 16; X, 3
Juice, choleric, XIII, 33
—softening, III, 8
—superfluous, II, 1; XII, 6, 8
—thick, III, 2; VI, 3; IX, 2; X, 2;
    XII, 8; XIII, 38
—thin, IX, 2
—vital, X, 8; XIII, 11, 25

Julep, VII, 2; XII, 1, 8

"Kamka," IX, 12
Kidneys, V, 6; IX, 2
Kurkuma, VII, 2
Kusbarath albir, VII, 2

Lavendula-stoechas, XII, 1
Laxatives, IX, 6; XI, 4; XII, 9;
    XIII, 32, 41
Leaven, III, 1
Leaves, VIII, 1
Leek, III, 3; IX, 12, 13
Lemonade, III, 4; IX, 3, 14, 15
Lemon juice, III, 9; IX, 1
Lentils, III, 3; VII, 2
Lethargy, V, 6; XIII, 36
Lettuce, III, 8
Lillium candidum, XII, 5, 8
Linseed, VII, 2; IX, 7, 8; XII, 5
Liquiritia glabria, VII, 3; XII, 1,
    2, 4, 5
Liver, II, 1; III, 1; IV, 3; V, 5, 6;
    VII, 4; IX, 2; XIII, 1, 36
Luck, VIII, 3
Lumbago, I, 1
Lungs, II, 2; III, 10; IV, 3; VII, 2;
    IX, 2; IX, 1; XII, 8

Macaroni, III, 1
Magic cure, PR., 1
Mallow, III, 8
Marakesh, XIII, 38
Marrow, IV, 6
Marubium Vulgare, XIII, 1, 3, 5,
    8
Massaging, I, 3; X, 5, 6, 7; XIII,
    15
Mastix, VII, 2; XIII, 6, 9
Mathematics, XIII, 13
Matsuts soup, IV, 4
Mead, VII, 2
Meat Jelly, III, 2
Meats, III, 3, 6, 7; IV, 4
Melongena, IV, 1
Memory, loss of, XIII, 3
Mental activity, VIII, 2
Mental debility, X, 8

112

114